LES CANADIENS

BOOKS BY ANDY O'BRIEN

Rocket Richard

Headline Hockey

Daredevils of Niagara

Fire-Wagon Hockey

Hockey Wingman

Young Hockey Champions

My Friend The Hangman

This Was My Choice (in collaboration with Igor Gouzenko)

To Darling Jay
from Mimi

"LES CANADIENS" the 1971 Playoff Giant-Killers.

FIRST ROW: Al MacNeil, John Ferguson, Sam Pollock, David Molson, Jean Béliveau, William Molson, Peter Molson, Henri Richard, Ronald Caron.

SECOND ROW: Rogatien Vachon, Bob Sheehan, Claude Larose, Marc Tardif, Jean-Claude Tremblay, Réjean Houle, Jacques Lemaire, Yvan Cournoyer.

THIRD ROW: Frank Mahovlich, Léon Rochefort, Phil Roberto, Ken Dryden, Terry Harper, Guy Lapointe, Philippe Myre.

BACK ROW: Yvon Bélanger, Larry Pleau, Peter Mahovlich, Pierre Bouchard, Jacques Laperrière, Serge Savard, Phil Langlois, Eddie Palchak.

Montreal *vs* Chicago 1971.

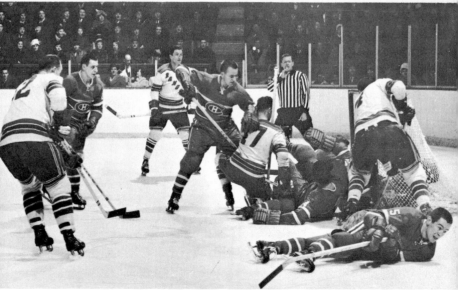

John Ambrose O'Brien, founder of the Canadiens.

Senator H. de M. Molson (cigarette), chairman of the board, and President J. David Molson (R) with author (L).

Typical fire-wagon rush. Canadiens pile up at Ranger net.

Joe Malone. Canadiens bought him from Quebec Bulldogs when NHL was formed in 1917. Scored 379 pro goals.

Howie Morenz was the "Babe Ruth of Hockey."

Newsy Lalonde, first Canadien super-star, remained a hot fan at the Forum until his death in 1970 at age 83.

LES CANADIENS

THE STORY OF THE MONTREAL CANADIENS

BY ANDY O'BRIEN

McGRAW-HILL RYERSON LIMITED
Toronto   Montreal   New York   London   Sydney
Johannesburg   Mexico   Panama   Düsseldorf   Singapore
Rio de Janeiro   Kuala Lumpur   New Delhi

DEDICATED TO A TRADITION

. . . the tradition of "fire-wagon" hockey that has kept Montreal's Canadiens a continuing symbol of story and spectacle throughout the dramatic fifty-four-year history of the National Hockey League.

PHOTOGRAPHY

Jacket cover and frontispiece: Macdonald Tobacco Company. Other photographs: David Bier; Turofsky; Jacques Lemercier; Roger St. Jean; Frank Prazak; Denis Brodeur

Les Canadiens
(Revised, previously published under the title Fire-Wagon Hockey)
Copyright © McGraw-Hill Ryerson Limited, 1971

ISBN 0-07-092950-9

1 2 3 4 5 6 7 8 9   AP-71   9 8 7 6 5 4 3 2 1

Printed and bound in Canada

Prologue

Shortly after midnight on May 18, 1971, I sat down at my typewriter because I found myself—a veteran observer of at least thirty-five Stanley Cup finals—too utterly hockey-spent and emotionally jazzed-up to sleep. Drama and turbulence and madcap skating had always been trademarks of *Le Club de Hockey Canadien Inc.* but this wackiest of all seasons had ended with a script no sane fiction editor would accept. And now I had a pressing assignment to write the story; perhaps in this period of sleepless calm after the storm I could collect my thoughts.

The editor-in-chief at McGraw-Hill Ryerson had rushed a request to update Canadiens' saga of fire-wagon hockey that I had put into a book in 1967 to mark the team's contribution on the fiftieth birthday of the National Hockey League.

But so much had been added to Canadiens' history since then—Could it possibly have happened in only four years?

Then it struck me: in those four years the Flying Frenchmen had won three Stanley Cups—three world championships—which was as many as New York Rangers and Chicago Black Hawks had each managed to win in their entire N.H.L. history dating back to 1926.

v

The mighty Boston Bruins, first American entry into the N.H.L. back in 1924, had won the Cup only four times.

This blazing interim had to be added to the half-century story but I was overwhelmed by a sensation of having experienced a hockey lifetime within the last forty days when Canadiens fought their way through twenty playoff games, all the way from an underdog No. 4 team rating after the regular season schedule to world champs. They surged amid ice crises to which were added bizarre off-ice crises causing headlines to bump into one another as red-eyed hockey writers dreaded to pick up a rival paper.

And now my typewriter was staring at me, impatiently.

I had to start somewhere—well, why not with the knockout, The Big Goal, the one that had lifted the Stanley Cup from the depths of apparently sure defeat. The 3—2 goal after Chicago Hawks' good-as-gold, 2—0 lead vanished in the last game of the longest-ever N.H.L. season.

The climax of the comeback had come at 2.34 of the third period as Henri Richard stilled the screaming thousands in Chicago Stadium with one of those breath-taking, beyond-doubt, homerun-type scores.

Team mate Jacques Lemaire had snapped up a loose puck beside the Chicago net and whipped it back to the onrushing Richard, who reached it just inside the Chicago blueline, but Richard seemingly lost the puck in his skates. Was it that moment of lost control that caused Chicago defenceman Keith Magnuson to let up for just a second or so? We will never know; in such furious action I doubt if Magnuson himself knows, but as Richard flipped the puck up from his skates to his stick Magnuson made a frantic lunge, plunging to the ice as Richard whipped around him in a blur of red, white and blue.

Chicago goaler Tony Esposito, winner of the 1970 top goaler award by a shoo-in, played it smartly by swooping outside his crease to cut down Richard's angle . . . but Richard didn't shoot.

Of course, we're now talking of split-second action. They tell you a goalie shouldn't make the first move but, dammit, Richard was directly ahead and only feet away. Esposito dropped to his knees to smother the rubber and I don't fault him on the move—it was the normal thing to do. But this Richard isn't exactly a normal type of player; here is his own terse explanation of what happened:

"After I managed to get around Magnuson I found myself right in there with Esposito. He came out and went down. I put it up, that's all."

I paused, staring at the typewriter. It was now well into the wee hours and by now I should be sleepy but, instead, another tingling memory was stirring—something familiar about the 3–2 goal . . . like watching a late, late TV movie . . . haven't I seen this before?

Reaching up to a bookshelf, I took down the book I had written on Canadiens' first half-century in the N.H.L. and looked wide-eyed at the opening chapter. About the 3–2 goal that won the 1966 Stanley Cup for Canadiens at the Detroit Olympia . . . The scorer? From flat on the ice, it was Henri Richard!

Nothing really had changed.

ANDY O'BRIEN

Illustrations

Contents

LES CANADIENS

Detroit Olympia: May 5, 1966

It was a sudden-death playoff situation.

The 1966 final series for the Stanley Cup, emblematic of the world's championship in the hockey Big Time, had gone to a sixth game in the best-of-seven series. In the five previous games, Canadiens had won three, Detroit Red Wings two. Regulation time in the sixth game had ended in a 2-2 tie; now it was overtime and the first goal would win the game.

For the Canadiens, a goal would mean the Cup. For Detroit, a goal would mean survival, forcing a seventh and final fray. The difference between winning and losing a final series also means a four-figure bundle of dollars per player.

At two minutes and twenty seconds of overtime, Canadiens rushed the Detroit end all-out. Defenceman Jean-Guy Talbot got the puck up to left winger Dave Balon who lifted a pass over Detroit defenceman Gary Bergman's stick.

Canadien centre Henri Richard, skating in high gear, made a desperate lunging effort to deflect the puck just as Bergman got a piece of him and sent Henri plunging head-first to the ice.

What happened next was vague at the time. Even the

dressing-room post-mortems were vague, but thank heavens for sequence-action cameras.

As Henri, stomach down on the ice, whizzed across the left corner of the Detroit net barely missing the post, the puck seemed to be riding on his outstretched right arm. There was an inches-wide opening between goalie Roger Crozier and the post; into that absurdly small opening went the puck off Henri's arm—or was it his leg by this time? Anyway, the puck slid to a stop a hair's width across the goal line.

There was a stunned moment of indecision. The capacity crowd in the Olympia stood wide-eyed with bated breath. No light had been turned on by the goal judge; the rules demand that the puck completely clear the goal line to be a goal and from the rear it didn't seem to be clear.

Referee Frank Udvari had sped into position, saw the puck was across but realized in a flash that this was the toughest decision of his fifteen National Hockey League years behind a whistle. If Richard had shoved the puck with arm or leg, it was an illegal goal; if, in Udvari's opinion, the puck had simply been deflected into the net by Henri's body, it meant the world's championship for Canadiens.

But into that moment of indecision was injected a flash of quick thinking that still rates as top, real-pro stuff with me. Behind the Canadiens' bench, Coach Toe Blake shrieked:

"Onto the ice . . . everybody yell . . . everybody!"

The Canadiens' bench exploded into loud jubilation. Out near the goal, Jean-Guy Talbot took the cue and went into an Indian war dance, arms and stick upraised. Richard, slightly fuzzy after crashing headlong into the boards behind the net, yelled automatically.

To this day, Udvari, now supervisor of NHL officials, won't admit that the noisy jubilation of the onrushing few among the silent sixteen thousand in the Olympia influenced his call but up went his arm. It was a goal!

No, it wasn't the clean-cut type of a score coming after a dramatic rush and a blistering shot that would deserve the world-championship tag.

Yes, it was on the "flukey" side.

But the whole episode—the whole package of melee action and lightning thinking behind the bench—added up to fire-wagon hockey. Canadiens, in their madcap, speed-crazy, hellbent approach to the game, have never really cared how the puck goes in.

Start of a Saga

An eight-column headline in The Montreal Star *of January 5, 1910, read:* $2,000 FINE AND SIXTY DAYS JAIL FOR PITRE IF HE PLAYS.

Thus was heralded the debut of Le Club de Hockey Canadien Inc. *An upstart newcomer to the ranks of an upstart second professional league, the National Hockey Association, Canadiens were born in a storm that has abated at times down through the years—but never for long. Excitement, controversy, headlines and rich servings of skill* sur la glace *seem to have been the team's preordained birthright.*

The dramatic Didier Pitre, often likened to an angry buffalo with a charging shot, did defy a court injunction that night at Montreal's old Jubilee Rink. The joint was jammed. The game against a seasoned Cobalt team from Ontario's booming silver mining belt was a screamer all the way. The newly-born Canadiens, after blowing a 3-0 lead, came from behind a 6-4 score to tie the game in regulation time and go on to win, 7-6, in the ninth minute of overtime.

But let's pause to thumb through the pages of the same newspaper quoted above.

The English and Scotch Woollen Company had a big

advertisement: "DON'T BE A HAND-ME-DOWN MAN." It went on to say that the day of the ready-made suit was over and proclaimed a made-to-order sale of suits and overcoats in imported woollens for fifteen dollars.

Another ad said: "His Grace the Archbishop of Quebec Strongly Recommends the Dr. John M. Mackay treatment for Drunkenness." Women's coats were on sale at W. H. Scroggie's, corner of St. Catherine and Peel, for $3.98. A ninety-seven-piece dinner-set sale special was priced at $4.79. A picture of a man pointing at YOU was located above the large-type query. "WOULD YOU LIKE TO MAKE MONEY?" It went on to explain that shares in the California-Alberta Oil Company could be bought at present for twenty-five cents although "in a few days the price will be raised to forty cents."

Sir Wilfrid Laurier, Prime Minister of Canada, had made a speech in Toronto the night before in which he did "not believe there is any danger from Germany." William Howard Taft, President of the United States, made an item or two as did Prime Minister Herbert Asquith of Britain. Jack Johnson, who had upended Canada's Tommy Burns for the world heavyweight title in 1908, was still champ.

That then was the era when hockey's most fabulous team entered, in what appears today an astonishingly off-hand fashion. In fact, the first franchise for the team now carrying a price tag of ten million dollars-plus cost not a single cent!

To sum up without entering into a maze of detail: a hockey war had developed in the ranks of the Eastern Canadian Hockey Association in late 1909. It concerned the natural-ice Jubilee Rink (located in Montreal's East End) which had bought the Montreal Wanderers' franchise. The ECHA, then hockey's top professional league, decided to play at the larger Westmount Arena (with the rink operators getting sixty per cent of the receipts).

To freeze out Wanderers, the ECHA executive simply

voted their league out of existence and formed a new one, the Canadian Hockey Association. Franchises were granted Ottawa, Shamrocks, Quebec, Nationals and All-Montreal—leaving Wanderers out in the cold without a league.

The initiation fee for clubs was set at thirty dollars with an annual subscription of twenty-five dollars. (Compare that with the National Hockey League expansion of 1967/68 where the six new clubs had to pay two million dollars each to enter.)

On that chill November 25, 1909, J. Ambrose O'Brien, son of M. J. O'Brien of Renfrew (who was later appointed senator), was in Montreal buying supplies for a railway contract on the St. Maurice River. He also owned the Cobalt and Haileybury teams in the miners-supported, rip-snorting Temiskaming League. He received a phone call from the owners (George and Jim Barnett) of the Renfrew Millionaires, suggesting that he apply for a franchise in the established league, renamed the Canadian Hockey Association.

This is Ambrose O'Brien's recollection of what happened when he did apply:

"My application was laughed at in Room 135 of the Windsor Hotel where the new CHA was meeting. Out in the hall I ran into General Manager J. Gardner of the Wanderers who said: 'Why don't we form a new league —you own Cobalt and Haileybury and represent Renfrew, while I have Wanderers?' So we held a meeting in Room 129."

At that meeting, Gardner had another idea. He said to O'Brien:

"Why don't you get together a French team here in Montreal to balance off Wanderers with French-English rivalry."

O'Brien, surprised, replied: "But I don't know any French players here."

"So what?" came back Gardner, "I do. In fact all

you'd have to do is back Jack Laviolette financially and the team will be formed for you."

So the National Hockey Association came into being in Room 129—made up of Wanderers, Renfrew, Cobalt, Haileybury and a team to be known as Les Canadiens.

A complication developed when the Renfrew owners, the Barnett Brothers, decided against going along with the new league and pulled out. J. Ambrose O'Brien* settled the problem without batting an eyelash—he simply took over the ownership of the Renfrew Millionaires, backed by the bankroll of his father, M. J. O'Brien, who donated a trophy to be awarded annually to the NHA Champions. Now out of competition and on display at the Hockey Hall of Fame, it is literally worth its weight in silver—the O'Brien Trophy was made of solid silver by Hemsley's of Montreal with silver mined at Cobalt.

(The ownership of four of the five teams in the new NHA by one man would really have shaken the latter-day critics of the National Hockey League who called it "the Norris House League" because two multi-millionaire brothers were involved at the same time. The late James Norris was a co-owner of the Chicago Black Hawks as well as being an owner of Madison Square Garden, home of the New York Rangers, while Bruce Norris was a co-owner of the Detroit Red Wings.)

J. Ambrose O'Brien told me: "My total investment in forming the great Canadiens club was five thousand dollars. I paid nothing for the franchise; that amount was for expenses including guaranteeing of player salaries. The understanding was that the Canadiens' franchise would be turned over to French sportsmen in Montreal

---

*Confusion between J. Ambrose O'Brien and the author often enters because of an interesting coincidence. Both were born in Renfrew, Ont. When Ambrose took over the Millionaires, the author's late father, Bill O'Brien, was the team trainer. Bill had started a thirty-year career as a major league trainer extending through the NHL to baseball's Brooklyn Dodgers. But the two O'Brien families are not related.

as soon as practicable." (The O'Brien interests withdrew from hockey two years later.)

Jack Laviolette seized the opportunity with greatest gusto. A noted hockey player himself as well as a colourful auto racer, his Jack's Cage on Notre Dame Street had long been a gathering place for players and he even had a team formed to play exhibition games.

For the new Canadiens' first game on January 5, 1910, Laviolette came up with a remarkable team. Those were the days of seven-man hockey and two thirty-minute periods.

He placed himself at the point position. For goal he got Joe Cattarinich who also served as team general manager (he was later an owner). He raided Nationals of the opposing league for Didier Pitre at cover. He signed at rover position the legendary Newsy Lalonde to a contract for the season calling for $1,300—quite a contrast to the NHL of today where the average salary with bonuses, added incentive money for league positional standing and playoff winnings, as well as special awards, nudges the twenty-thousand-dollar mark.

Ed Décarie was centre, Art Bernier and Skinner Poulin were the wings on that starting team. One of the subs was Richard Duckett who later became Coroner of Montreal.

Getting back to the headline at the start of this chapter: it related to an injunction taken out by the raging Nationals in an effort to stop Didier Pitre from appearing with Canadiens. A distinguished Montreal lawyer, Harry J. Trihey, had publicly warned that if Pitre dared set a skate on the ice at the Jubilee Rink that night he would be liable to a fine of $2,000 and six months imprisonment.

The hockey war was now on; and, since all's fair in love and war, the Laviolette approach to the Pitre problem was presumably justified. When Pitre pointed out that he had signed to play for the Nationals for $1,100,

Laviolette offered him $1,700 "spot cash" and agreed—
if the courts forced Pitre back to Nationals—to forget
about the $1,700. In other words, Pitre could end up
with an awesome total for that era of $2,800. (Pitre
eventually stayed on with the Canadiens; the legal problem dissolved.)

The Canadiens' debut caught Montreal's fancy in a
vigorous way—the Jubilee Rink was bulging at the seams
with hundreds turned away. I enjoyed the ecstatic quality
of the Montreal *Star's* coverage so much that here is the
account verbatim—without byline; bylines weren't yet
in vogue:

Five thousand men and women and young people,
goading the players by voice and cheers, derisive yells
and tumultuous and overwhelming encomiums, precisely
as did other people (long since dust and ashes) their
young athletes for the sake of strength and beauty; fourteen young men battling for victory with as much passion
and eagerness as was ever expressed in war; a tension
painful in its acuteness; a struggle which took every
ounce of power and endurance, every atom of skill, out
of as athletic a set of fellows as could be imagined; an
enormous expectancy which communicated itself to every
soul in the Jubilee Rink. and which became, as the
struggle progressed, well-nigh intolerable—this was the
match, this the hockey, these the conditions which
marked the initial contest between the Canadiens and
the Cobalts and which resulted in a victory for the
Canadiens by 7 goals to 6.

As water unto wine must be deemed all that has gone
before this season. No doubt last impressions are most
vivid but veteran players, many of whom came from all
parts of the city to watch the game, avowed that for
speed, even balance, furious rushes, tension, skill and
combination play the match has rarely been surpassed,
if indeed it has been equalled by the great matches which
the old players love to recount, as the veteran soldier
shoulders his crutch and "shows how fields are won."

If from the above you deduce that it must have been quite a hockey game, we've both reached the same conclusion. The account went on to talk of "frightful collisions," considerable "hurt and blood," stoppages of the play and "temporary retirement of disabled players." Lalonde, Poulin and Bernier bagged two goals apiece and Laviolette the other.

Edouard Charles (Newsy) Lalonde was the first superstar of the Canadiens—so it's an historical fact that the team had one of the Exalted Fraternity from the very first game. Besides being an elected member of the Hocky Hall of Fame, he was also voted in a 1950 Canadian Press poll as the outstanding lacrosse player of the half-century.

Newsy's storied playing career extended over twenty-one seasons in professional hockey leading up to Stanley Cup competition. They were divided, between 1905 and 1927, among teams representing Cornwall, Toronto, Renfrew, Montreal's Canadiens, Vancouver, the Canadiens again, Saskatoon and the New York Americans. For two and a half seasons, between 1932 and 1935, he coached the Canadiens.

When he was elected to the Hockey Hall of Fame, the publicity releases concentrated on Newsy's scoring savvy which got him 441 goals in 365 pro games and left him five times leading scorer in various leagues. But oldtimers seem more in awe of the bloody duels he had with such players as Joe Hall.

Hall, as a star of Quebec Bulldogs, had nearly severed Newsy's windpipe in Quebec. The next game in Montreal saw blood-hungry crowds batter down the gates of the old Westmount Arena where Hall promptly carved Newsy for eighteen stitches. As soon as the doctor got him tied together again, Newsy returned to the ice and shattered Hall's collarbone.

"But there was nothing personal about it", Newsy told me in 1967 when, at the age of seventy-nine, he was moaning about a broken hip forcing him to give up bowling, "When Hall later joined Canadiens we became friends and roomies."

Getting back to Canadiens' first season, they ended last in the seven-team league. Seven teams? Things did get somewhat confusing when, with the NHA schedule under way, the Ottawa team and Shamrocks of Montreal jumped the Canadian Hockey Association and joined the National Hockey Association.

It is also typical of the rather fluid way that hockey organizations operated in the era that, toward the end of the campaign, when Renfrew was making a desperate bid to catch Wanderers and Ottawa, the Renfrew team obtained Newsy Lalonde from the out-of-it Canadiens for the remaining games. It was easy to arrange because J. Ambrose O'Brien owned both teams.

Wanderers eventually copped the Cup but Newsy emerged as scoring champion; in a total of eleven games played with Canadiens and Renfrew he scored thirty-eight goals. In one game with Renfrew he scored nine goals.

It took Canadiens six years to build from the NHA bottom to the Stanley Cup top.

The first step had already been taken in getting Lalonde. The next step was the signing of a twenty-year-old goalkeeper in Chicoutimi, Que., named Georges Vezina, for the team's second season.

From the very start he was a sensation. His coolness under fire in those days when a goaler wasn't allowed to go down to save (the rule wasn't changed until 1922) soon won him the superb moniker, "Chicoutimi Cucumber."

Canadiens finished second in 1911 to Ottawa (who went on to win the Cup), as Vezina dominated a sterling array of goalers—Percy Lesueur of Ottawa, Riley Hern of Wanderers, Paddy Moran of Quebec and Bert Lindsay of Renfrew. (Lindsay was the father of Ted Lindsay, now retired Detroit Red Wings immortal and Hall of Famer.)

Vezina's first season saw him give up an average of 3.9 goals in sixteen games played. He played a total of three hundred and seventy-three consecutive games for Canadiens, averaging 3.49 a game, up to the end of the first period against Pittsburgh on November 28, 1925, when he was forced to retire with a temperature and severe chest pains. Vezina was fatally stricken with tuberculosis; his memory is perpetuated not only in the Hall of Fame but also in the Vezina Trophy awarded annually to hockey's top puck-stopper.

Personally, I have one vivid memory of Vezina from the very first major hockey game I saw. It was in 1924 at the old Mount Royal Arena in Montreal. Babe Dye, owner of a shot, the violence of which wasn't duplicated until Bobby Hull came on the scene thirty-three years later, got a breakaway down the centre alley. Vezina remained upright as a statue. At about thirty feet out, Dye leaned on one; only Vezina's left arm moved as he picked off the puck with almost disdainful ease.

On December 7, 1911, a bomb fell on pro hockey that was comparable in effect to the bombing of Pearl Harbor thirty years to the day later. The 1911 bomb unleashed an unprecedented hockey war; the Pacific Coast Hockey Association was formed at a meeting in Vancouver and declared the world would be its oyster in seeking talent.

Three teams formed the first league—Vancouver, Victoria and New Westminster. Of a total of twenty-three players for the three teams (despite playing seven-man rules) no less than sixteen were recruited from eastern clubs. One of the eastern stars wooed west was Canadiens' Newsy Lalonde.

Newsy won the PCHA scoring championship in its 1912 debut season but Canadiens traded for and got him back in the summer of that year. The avalanche of litigation and suspension evaporated, all was forgiven. Montreal was just plain glad to see him "home" again.

He was also just in time to play a key role in the introduction of the National Hockey Association to Toronto.

Two franchises had been given to the city—to the Toronto Blueshirts and to the Tecumsehs, later the Ontarios, later the Shamrocks—contingent upon the completion of a new arena there. The arena was late but finally opened on December 22, 1912, with an exhibition game between the Canadiens and the Montreal Wanderers.

With the Wanderers were the famed Cleghorn brothers, Odie and Sprague. Early in the game Newsy dumped Odie Cleghorn into the boards. Sprague, the tough 'un of the family, rushed over and bashed Newsy across the forehead with his stick for twelve stitches. Cleghorn was hauled into court the next day and fined fifty dollars for assault.

All Toronto was talking—about the NHA, which was exactly what was wanted.

Ownership of Canadiens shifted from J. Ambrose O'Brien to a Montreal wrestling promoter, George Kennedy, for $7,500. His name was really Kendall but, in taking up an early career as a wrestler, he had changed it because of violent objections from his father, a tough Scottish sea captain.

Kennedy was as tough as his background. In the files of the NHL today there is a letter of protest from a referee addressed to T. Emmett Quinn, then president of the NHA. In the letter, dated March 3, 1914, the referee described the assault made on him, physically and verbally, by Kennedy after Canadiens were defeated by Wanderers, 6-5, in overtime on February 28, 1914.

The referee was Leo Dandurand, later to become manager-coach of a Canadien Stanley Cup team.

The face of hockey was changing in the NHA. From two periods of thirty minutes it had been altered to three periods of twenty minutes in 1911. In 1912, the rover position was abolished, making it six-man hockey. Teams were ordered to have distinctive uniforms and to carry numbers. Players could now be changed at any time instead of waiting for the whistle.

New penalties were introduced, designed to clean up and speed up play, in 1913, carrying two-dollar fines on second offence. In 1914, referees were ordered to drop the puck instead of placing it on the ice. A goaler who deliberately left his feet, sprawling to save, would be fined two dollars the first time. The second time cost three dollars and a five-minute penalty. The third time five dollars and ten minutes. The fourth time cost ten dollars and a match penalty. Another interesting rule introduced that season kept teams at six-man strength throughout the game; a sub replaced a fellow player leaving the ice for a penalty or any other reason. In 1914 a puck rebounding off the goaler was no longer offside, and boarding was now deemed deserving of a major penalty.

That same year saw a Toronto sports promoter, Eddie Livingstone, pop into the NHA picture by taking over the Ontarios franchise—he promptly changed the name to Shamrocks.

The Toronto Blueshirts had matured rapidly and amazed the hockey world in winning the Stanley Cup for 1914 by knocking off Canadiens and Victoria.

Livingstone, who was to become an unwilling cause for the creation of the National Hockey League a few years later, proceeded to annex the Blueshirts as well in 1915. A stormy session of the NHA executive decided he could not operate two Toronto franchises (while J. Ambrose O'Brien owned four franchises, they had been spread over as many locales) and he was given until November twentieth to sell his Shamrock franchise.

Things were simplified for Livingstone when the PCHA raided the Toronto Blueshirts, leaving only a skeleton. He rebuilt the team around players under contract to his Shamrocks.

Meanwhile, another team was rebuilding in a big way. The Canadiens, after finishing in the cellar in 1915, pre-

sented a formidable array of new talent for 1916. Vezina
was still in goal and Lalonde at centre, flanked by Pitre
and Laviolette, who was moved up from defence. The
defence consisted of two new members, Howard Mc-
Namara and Goldie Prodgers, backed up by Bert Corbeau. Adding to bench depth were: Louis Berlinquette,
Skinner Poulin, Skene Ronan, Amos Arbour and Jack
Fournier.

While Canadiens had ended in the 1915 cellar, the
vaunted Ottawa Senators' powerhouse had gone west
and was heavily favoured to demolish the Vancouver
Millionaires. The result was a shocker to the east as
Vancouver swept the series by scores of 6-2, 8-3 and
12-3.

The 1916 season saw the Canadiens rise all the way
from the cellar and into the Stanley Cup finals but even
their faithful weren't free with betting money. The Vancouver team who had created such an atmosphere of
awe by their pulverizing of the Senators had been ousted
in the west by an even mightier array, the Portland Rosebuds.

The patched-up Canadiens, underdogs according to
the wise money, looked even more hopeless after the first
game in which they were goose-egged by the Rosebuds,
2-0. Canadiens rallied to win the second game, 2-1, and
went ahead with a 6-5 thriller win in the third game only
to have Portland tie the series with another 6-5 score in
the fourth fray.

The fifth and last game of the series was a squeaker—
Canadiens emerged on the healthy end of a 2-1 count
and the team took their first lusty quaffs of champagne
from the Stanley Cup.

Didier Pitre was the scoring star but it was generally
conceded, as it was to be conceded in so many springs
to come, that goaling spells the difference in a tight
series. The great Vezina was sensationally stingy, allowing an average of only 2.6 goals-against in the five games.

The series was played in Montreal at the Westmount

Arena (corner of St. Catherine Street and Wood Avenue, one block west of today's Forum) to which the Canadiens had moved from the ancient Jubilee Rink. They thus increased the seating capacity from three thousand to six thousand but a slight increase in prices (from $1.25 tops and 50 cents minimum) for the series was blamed for a disappointing take at the box office.

The breakdown looks ludicrous in this age.

The total revenue from the first three games in which the players shared was only $11,504. The arena deducted $3,834. The expenses guarantee to the visiting team took $2,500. The league's share was $555. The officials received $200. Which left each player of the winning Canadiens with $238 and each losing Rosebud with $208.

(Contrast that with today in the NHL: a team's take for ending atop the league, winning the semi-finals and the finals, could earn $5,750 per player—said amount being exclusive of his regular season pay, any All-Star bonus, trophy-winning bonus or any other added incentive money.)

The revenue from the last two games was split three ways, the club owners and the rink getting about $1,500 each.

To this drab financial finish was added an even drabber summer as enlistments in the armed forces riddled both the Eastern and Western leagues. Canadiens lost a quarter of their 1916 title team as their star defence duo of McNamara-Prodgers, and Arbour, donned khaki. Yet they made it into the 1917 Cup finals against Seattle Metropolitans, only to bow out in four games.

In losing, the Canadiens contributed in a back-door way to hockey history; this marked the Stanley Cup's first crossing of the border into possession of an American club.

The westward and downward departure of the Stanley Cup was only one of the many disquieting happenings to hit the NHA that season.

The 228th Battalion (also known as the Northern Fusiliers) had recruited so many good pro players that an application to enter the NHA had been made and accepted at a special league meeting in September, 1916. The soldier team was only slightly less than terrific—skating over Ottawa, Canadiens, Wanderers, Toronto and Quebec in turn. They were still very much the team to beat when they were ordered overseas and withdrew from the league on February tenth.

The NHA decided the schedule had been unbalanced by the departure of the 228th and solved the problem in another special meeting, on February 11th, by a curious decision typical of the times. To the horror and shouting indignation of Eddie Livingstone, it was decided to drop his Toronto team for the rest of the schedule, the players to be divided among the other teams. Two joined the 228th, two went to Ottawa, one to Canadiens; and Wanderers (after Quebec waived its rights to Wanderers) got three.

On February nineteenth, a furore erupted when it was charged that Eddie Oatman had not really enlisted in the 228th but had been hired to play hockey with the soldiers—he was discharged "for special circumstances" when the battalion got to St. John. Gordon Meeking was also discharged there as medically unfit and caused another furore by claiming he had been promised a commission to play hockey. He had worn an officer's uniform before leaving for St. John and been given a hero's send-off on leaving Toronto. The battalion officers hotly insisted that Meeking had been properly recruited and properly discharged, but public reaction was sour.

So ended the bleakest hours of the NHA in that winter of 1916/17. Everybody felt that before another NHA season opened—if it opened at all—something must happen. But nobody in those unsettled days could possibly have imagined how historically big that something would be.

The Infant Howled Lustily

The 1953 Stanley Cup finals shifted to Boston after the first two games in Montreal saw Canadiens and Bruins win one apiece. True to Beantown tradition, the Bruins tossed an all-out luncheon for the press. As General Manager Art Ross, our host, stood up, the younger writers saw a battle-scarred but somewhat venerable executive who they knew had taken over the brand-new Bruins of 1924 and built three Stanley Cup teams. The senior writers saw an intriguing link with hockey's yesteryear—a stormy star who had once been suspended from organized hockey for negotiating with the players of the old NHA for a proposed new league.

Now a salty Hall of Famer, he commented on "those curious quotes" we had been publishing from the rival coaches. Dick Irvin had gloomily given his Canadiens "little chance against the driving Bruins" while Bruins' Lynn Patrick, not to be outdone in psychological warfare, warned local fans to expect the worst.

"After reading those quotes, said Ross, "I wish to propose that the two teams switch coaches for the rest of the series."

The National Hockey League was born in anger. It was an open secret that the NHA executive was about to erupt because, as one oldtimer told me, "we were fed up with Eddie Livingstone shaking his fist under everybody's nose." When word got around that the other NHA owners were planning to get rid of Eddie by establishing a new league and leaving him out, the Toronto Arena directors hurriedly purchased the franchise from Eddie and made the rink manager, Charles Querrie, boss of the new franchise—if one was obtained.

The Westmount Arena was sick of NHA bickerings and said so. The Toronto picture had gone sour as a result of the previous season's withdrawals but, unbelievably, the Toronto Arena had the only artificial ice available. The Quebec Bulldogs had decided to pull out. Indeed, professional hockey was barely managing to keep its head above water in those dour days of World War I when today's powerful, immensely wealthy National Hockey League was born—with the infant howling lustily at the Windsor Hotel in Montreal on November 22, 1917.

What should have been the K.O. punch was thrown at the new league a bit more than a month later.

At the founding meeting it had been decided to launch the NHL with four franchises—Canadiens, Ottawa, Wanderers and Toronto Arenas. There was a brief uproar when Querrie resigned; the rumours had it that Livingstone was behind it although the franchise was granted only on condition that he wouldn't be running the team. The issue was settled within a week; Querrie was finally in full power.

Financial trouble was facing Wanderers from the start when the opener in Montreal (against Toronto) saw only seven hundred of the six thousand Westmount Arena seats filled. Then, on the night of January 2, 1918, the Arena burned down; with the blaze went all the equipment of both the Wanderers and the Canadiens.

Wanderers folded up—claiming a deficit of thirty thousand dollars.

Canadiens returned to the old Jubilee Rink and began hunting for new gear.

The NHL was now an extremely sick league, reduced to three teams, Toronto, Ottawa and Canadiens. But in the Canadiens' case the patient was doing more than "just breathing"; as their incomparably fervent French fans noted, the team had received an exciting shot in the arm thanks to the demise of the Quebec club. Canadiens got Newsy's old pet hate, Joe Hall, Joe Malone and three other players for only seven hundred dollars.

Joe Malone!

It could be that he averted Canadiens' demise. Hindsight tells us that the Wanderers goofed fatally in not picking him up—as last-place finishers the previous season the Wanderers had first choice at the Quebec grab-bag but passed over Malone, who had actually led the league in scoring during the previous season with forty-one goals in nineteen games.

Normally a centre, Malone was shifted over to the left wing with Newsy Lalonde at centre and Didier Pitre at right wing.

In the opening game, against Ottawa, Canadiens won, 7-4, with Malone scoring five goals from his "strange" position. He stayed there and went on to lead the league again—this time with forty-four goals, a record for a single season that stood for thirty-seven years until another Canadien, Rocket Richard, scored fifty. (Because Malone got his forty-four in 20 games whereas Rocket got fifty in fifty games, it would be fairer to list Malone's record as something still very much alive.)

Because of his quiet, non-violent, precision-type of play, Malone was an intriguing contrast even with line-mates Newsy and Didier. He was the key figure of Canadiens' exciting start in the National Hockey League's debut year.

Canadiens bowed out in a brutal, penalty-laden eastern playoff with Toronto but the following spring, 1920, they got by Ottawa in the east to face Seattle in the west for the Stanley Cup.

Once again Canadiens shared in NHL history that mixed spectacular hockey and tragedy.

It was agreed that the games would be played alternately under Western rules (the PCHA still played the seven-man game with rover added). Seattle, playing their own rules, swamped Canadiens, 7-0, in the opener. The second game, under Eastern rules, saw Canadiens win, 4-2, with Newsy Lalonde scoring all four.

The third game, back to Western rules, saw Newsy play his heart out in three positions—centre, rover and defence—as Canadiens lost, 7-2.

The fourth game was described as the greatest game ever seen to that date on the Pacific Coast. It ended in a scoreless tie after one hour and forty minutes of overtime.

The fifth game saw Canadiens finally solve the Western rules to win 4-2 with "Rover" Lalonde getting two. There the stern series ended with two wins apiece.

The Spanish influenza epidemic, sweeping the continent, had finally caught up with the playoffs. Joe Hall died in hospital. Lalonde and three other Canadiens were confined to their beds. Manager George Kennedy, badly stricken, never really recovered and died two years later.

The Stanley Cup series went into the record books as the only one ever abandoned with no winner declared for 1919.

Canadiens had done remarkably well during 1919 considering that they had Malone only for games played in Montreal during the regular season. He played in the Eastern playoffs against Ottawa but not at all against Seattle. While researching this book, I contacted Joe— now a hale and hearty seventy-seven-year-older, retired and enjoying it. He explained:

"I had hooked on to a good job in Quebec City which promised a secure future, something hockey in those days couldn't. I did score seven goals in the eight regular home

games in which I played and helped beat Ottawa, but my
heart sure bled while Newsy and the boys were battling
through that grim grind in Seattle. I have often wondered
if . . . but what's the use?"

What Malone wondered about was something Canadien fans were sure about—if Malone had been out there,
he would have made the difference in the scoreless tie and
Canadiens would have won in five games, making the
abandoned sixth game unnecessary.

The next season saw the Quebec Bulldogs revived and
all their former players ordered returned, including
Malone. This really hurt—especially after the tragic loss
of Joe Hall as well. With Malone, Canadiens could have
remained the team to beat in the East because, even
though the resurrected Bulldogs won only four games in
twenty-four starts in that season of 1920, Malone again
won the scoring crown with thirty-nine goals.

On January 31, 1920, against Toronto St. Pats (formerly the Arenas) his deadly shooting accounted for
seven goals—a single game record that still stands in the
NHL record books as this is written on the loop's fiftieth
Anniversary.

He also scored four in a game against Canadiens—the
fourth beating his old mates in overtime. Against Ottawa,
he almost equalled his own record with six goals.

Right behind Malone, with thirty-seven goals, was
Newsy Lalonde who came close to his mate's record with
six goals in a single game—Toronto again the patsies. An
odd row developed when Manager George Kennedy publicly accused Lalonde of "hogging the puck" in an effort
to beat out Malone. It was like the legendary medical
report about the operation being a success but the patient
dying—Canadiens out-scored Ottawa during both halves
of the schedule, yet Ottawa won both halves with more
wins, thus eliminating the need for an Eastern playoff.
Ottawa then knocked off Seattle for the Cup.

However, Canadiens did have something to show for

Pulsating moment in Canadiens' history at Forum, April 8, 1952.
Battered Bruin goalie Sugar Jim Henry shakes hand of bleeding,
still-wobbly Rocket.

When at long last the most-wanted player of all time, Jean
Beliveau, finally signed in 1953/54, general manager Frank
Selke (L) and Coach Dick Irvin (R) registered joy unconfined.
On June 9, 1971, Jean Beliveau retired after 18 seasons and
10 Stanley Cups to become vice-president and Director of
Corporate Relations—in other words, "official spokesman of the
Canadiens."

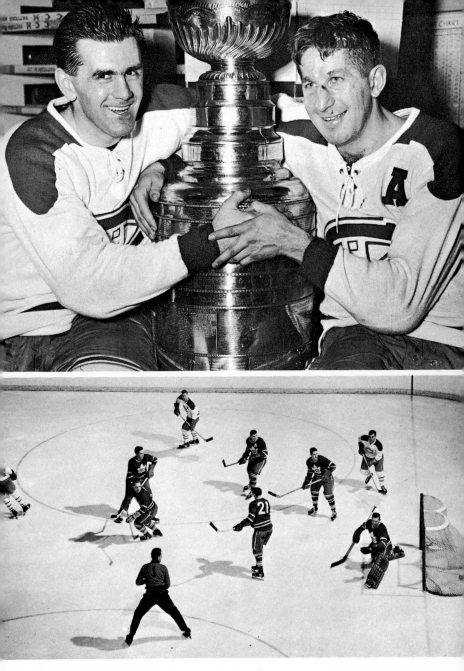

Richard and Lach with Stanley Cup.

Rocket scores on entire Toronto team, January 21, 1955.

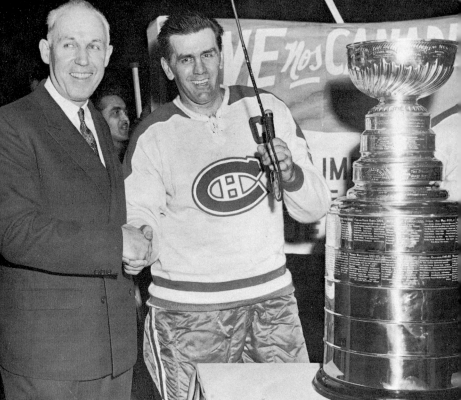

In the savage Richard Riot night of March 17, 1955, President Clarence Campbell was attacked by a black-jacketed hoodlum.

After Canadiens won the Stanley Cup in 1960, Campbell congratulated captain Rocket, who then ended his playing career.

the dazzling though ineffective season when they forgot
about hockey being more than an offensive game, that
cutting down on goals-against is important, too. They
finally had a new home, the Mount Royal Arena. And
just in time; the tired old Jubilee Rink, weary of com-
plaints about its age and size, joined Canadiens' previous
home by burning to ashes.

The opening of the Mount Royal Arena was a rousing
affair on the night of January tenth with the goal-crazy
Canadiens skating to a free-wheeling, 14-7 win over
Toronto before what was reported as "a capacity crowd
of six thousand." It could have been a bit too rousing.
Either that or the super-capacity crowd of sixty-five hundred reported at a game against Ottawa a week later must
have included Joe Btfsplk, the world's worst jinx. Halfway through the fray, part of the balcony collapsed.
Happily there were no serious casualties but the incident
must have unnerved the Canadiens; they won by only 3-2.

However, the rink-bulging crowds were taking on significance. A record was set in the east at the Toronto
Arena as eighty-five hundred fans turned out one night
while, at the Vancouver Arena in the west, over nine
thousand paid to see another game. And the box office
began to get daring; when Seattle Mets came east for the
Stanley Cup finals at Ottawa, they found tickets raised to
an unprecedented tops of $2.20 (with a fifty-five cent
minimum). And all-night queues of fans waiting to pick
them up.

It had also become apparent that the spines of both
leagues had become stiffened by the strength of presidents
whose gradual assumption of real authority was injecting
order into what had been something just short of hockey
chaos. The NHL had made a former sports writer and
NHA secretary, Frank Calder, its president. The PCHA
had firmly installed ex-star Frank Patrick as its boss.
While Patrick had held the post since 1913 and Calder

since the NHL's birth in 1917, they were now being allowed more bite than bark.

The 1920/21 season again saw Canadiens plod through behind the thirty-two-goal scoring of its ice leader, Newsy Lalonde, but a new scoring sensation had taken over. He was Cecil (Babe) Dye of Toronto St. Pats whose bullet shot totalled thiry-five goals. Quebec had pulled out of the NHL again—this time permanently— and the franchise shifted to Hamilton.

Canadiens did share profitably in one headline game that season. It was a typical Montreal rhubarb game on January twenty-sixth—the start of the NHL second half (the league played two halves in those days, with the winner of each eventually playing off to face the Western opponent for the Stanley Cup). Canadiens were leading Ottawa, 5-3, when, with less than six minutes to go, the Ottawa team stomped off the ice in anger and refused to play any more. The game was forfeited to Canadiens, and Ottawa, top team of the first half of the schedule, went on to lose a total of seven straight games.

I have always thought of that 1920/21 season as a classic warning to hockey coaches and teams never to give up or adopt a "wait until next season" attitude.

Because of their grim showing in the second half, Ottawa Senators weren't given a ghost of a chance against Toronto in the Eastern playoffs, yet they bounced up with an upset 5-0 win in the first of the two-game, total-goals series. It was enough to carry them through despite Toronto's 2-0 win the second game.

When Ottawa went west for the Cup finals, Vancouver scented a victory because of Ottawa's seasonal record and the largest crowd up to that time in Canadian hockey history, eleven thousand, turned out to see their team win as expected. But Ottawa came back with a pair of wins. Vancouver evened up the series and Ottawa took the fifth for the championship, although playing a man short because of penalties during almost the entire game.

All five games were won by a single-goal margin and a total of fifty-one thousand tickets were sold.

The year 1921 marked the passing of Canadiens' owner, George Kennedy. In addition to his major revenue from wrestling, the great sports promoter had said he never made less than ten thousand dollars a season profit out of Canadiens, which established the club's sale price of $11,500 as an impressive bargain for the new owners. The combination was made up of ex-referee Leo Dandurand; Joe Cattarinich, who had been goaler of the first Canadiens team back in 1910, and a Montreal sportsman, Louis Letourneau. (Incidentally, they outbid Frank Calder who had offered ten thousand dollars.)

The first Canadiens' franchise had cost J. Ambrose O'Brien nothing. After spending five thousand dollars on the team he sold it to Kennedy for seventy-five hundred dollars.

The three-way combine paid eleven thousand five hundred dollars in 1921 and sold it in 1935 to a group of Montreal financiers (headed by Ernie Savard, Maurice Forget and Louis Gelinas) for one hundred and sixty-five thousand dollars. Not a bad profit within a fourteen-year span.

Just how the next sale went and for how much is uncertain.

Senator Donat Raymond was president of the Canadien Arena Company that financed the construction of what was in 1924 the largest indoor arena in North America, the Montreal Forum. It immediately became the home of the new Montreal Maroons, and the Canadiens moved in as tenants the next year, 1925. At first all looked rosy but then came the Lean Thirties.

The Maroons folded in 1938. The crowds dwindled badly and NHL hockey in Montreal was fighting for survival until Senator Raymond assumed control of the Canadiens from the Savard syndicate and turned his financial strength to another team-rebuilding job.

In 1957 Senator Raymond sold out—Canadiens and
Forum—to the immensely prestigious and wealthy Molson family for a reported four million dollars. Recently,
while trying to work out a probable value of the Forum-
Canadiens operation, I was told that a would-be buyer
would have to start his bidding with ten million dollars.

To J. Ambrose O'Brien goes my award for the all-time
understatement of sports history when he wryly commented to me in 1967: "I guess I sold out a bit too soon."

But let's flip back to the 1921 take-over. Besides being
in on the owning, Leo Dandurand took over as manager-
coach with an avowed purpose that set the pattern for
Canadiens for years to come. He went out to build a team
capable of more than skilled play.

"The way I see hockey," he told the press, "no team
can hope to achieve world championship status in this
high-speed, physical contact game unless it can not only
out-play opposing teams but physically overwhelm them
as well. Down in their hearts they should feel that they
can beat the opposition in the alley as well as on the ice.
I don't want hockey hoodlums but I do want he-man
hockey talent that can meet any and all situations. That's
the game to me, that's how the Canadiens will play."

Dandurand's first move in that direction was to get
Sprague Cleghorn, a rock-ribbed defenceman who had
finished up the previous season with Ottawa by drawing
four penalties (the last one a match penalty) in the Cup
final at Vancouver. It took a three-for-two trade to get
him from Hamilton, whose property he had become
through an exchange of player properties too complicated
to warrant space here. But it seemed right that he should
shift to Canadiens; Sprague was born in Montreal and
his brother, Odie, was already on the team. Besides,
Montreal fans have always liked their hockey dishes
served with lots of spice.

A great team was building with the addition of another

newcomer, Billy Boucher. They joined proven stalwarts: Vezina, Lalonde, Pitre, Berlinquette, Bert Corbeau and Odie Cleghorn.

Looking back, it is easy to criticize the way emphasis on hard hockey resulted in harsh hockey but all of Canada developed harshly. The thinking then wouldn't be acceptable in the modern era yet there is no denying that the turbulent Canadiens developed a vigorous following.

There was turbulence within and without.

Within the team ranks, Newsy Lalonde resigned after a dispute with Dandurand.

"For the first time in my hockey life," raged Lalonde, "I have been accused of not giving my best."

President Calder intervened and Lalonde returned after an absence of four games during which, significantly, Dandurand had appointed Sprague Cleghorn as a sort of "ice general."

Sprague's idea of generalship was rather basic. In a game at Ottawa on February first, he and brother Odie made a shambles of the opposition—three Ottawa stars, Eddie Gerard, Frank Nighbor and Cy Denneny, were knocked out of action for the next two games. Referee Lou Marsh publicly classed the Cleghorns "a disgrace to hockey." Ottawa formally requested that Sprague be expelled from the game but President Calder shrugged off the request.

When Canadiens and Ottawa next met it was at the Mount Royal Arena in Montreal. It ended in a 6-6 tie and Newsy Lalonde was booed by the crowd for failing to come up with the winning goal on what seemed "a sure thing breakaway."

Three weeks later, when Canadiens just missed second place and the playoffs (the split-schedule had been abolished in favor of a system in which the first and second team would play off for the Eastern title), Newsy played his last game with Canadiens.

Before the next season opened, Dandurand made a trade that brought about the return of Joe Malone (from Hamilton) but everybody knew Joe was fading badly.

Then Dandurand came up with another trade that shocked Montreal fans to the core. Rugged Newsy Lalonde was shipped to Saskatoon in exchange for a frail, Ottawa-born amateur under option to Saskatoon. The one-hundred-and-forty-pound kid's name was Aurel Joliat.

The angry discussion raged until the Canadiens' opening game in Toronto when the unlikely Canadien rookie bagged two slick goals. Billy Boucher, Odie Cleghorn and Joliat ended as 1-2-3- Canadien scorers as they made it into the two-game, total-points Eastern playoff with Ottawa.

In the first game the old bitterness boiled up at the Mount Royal Arena into a general riot. Ottawa's Cy Denneny suffered a concussion when knocked out by Billy Couture's stick and Sprague Cleghorn crosschecked Lionel Hitchman across the face, knocking him out. Both Couture and Cleghorn drew match penalties from Referee Lou Marsh who was assaulted by fans charging the ice as "bottles showered like confetti." Tommy Gorman (then Ottawa manager and a conscientious Catholic) was also mobbed by fans calling him a "blankety-blank Orangeman from Ottawa."

General Sir Arthur Currie, then principal of McGill University and former Commander of the Canadian Corps overseas, was so horrified by the cutting-down display that he issued a statement next day:

"I would rather see every grandstand in the country burned down than a repetition of the disgraceful scenes of last night."

Although Canadiens had lost 2-0, in that first game, the cagey Dandurand decided to beat Calder to the draw by an unprecedented move—Dandurand himself suspended both Cleghorn and Couture for the rest of the series.

Frankly, I believe Dandurand figured he would lose his stalwart pair for only the other Ottawa game by his do-it-yourself action whereas Calder might have suspended his players for the rest of the season.

As it happened, Canadiens won, 2-1, and lost the Eastern playoffs by one goal. Justice triumphed in that Cy Denneny scored the single counter that eliminated Canadiens. And Ottawa went on to win the 1923 Cup.

Sprague Cleghorn seemed amazed by his election to the Hockey Hall of Fame in 1958 but was also delightfully unrepentant in an interview I had with him when the news broke. He admitted to disabling the three Ottawa players on the night in 1922, and when I asked how many hockey fights he'd been in, Sprague asked:

"Do you mean stretcher-case fights?"

I could only nod.

"I guess I've been in 50 of those kind," he said.

He was fond of Newsy Lalonde for a particular reason. "After I was arrested for almost killing him one night in Toronto, Newsy turned up in court next morning to plead for me and I got off with a two hundred dollar fine."

If all this gives the impression that I'm trying to whitewash outrageously harsh hockey, I certainly am not. But Canadiens were never dull. Rightly or wrongly, for better or for worse, they have occupied headlines throughout their career as hockey's oldest professional club.

Violent play alone couldn't have held fan interest. They produced breathtaking thrills in the strict hockey sense and one intriguing angle was already apparent.

Somehow they always come up with a superstar. The superstar has a magical draw. The Montreal Maroons won their second Stanley Cup in 1935 yet died three seasons later because they had only—yes, only—a great team. Fans grow weary of a machine because they can't identify themselves with a machine but the superstar gets "adopted" in the public mind, to be cheered, to be jeered, to be protected against critics, to be alibied if necessary.

When Canadiens had both Newsy Lalonde and Joe Malone, the Montreal fans were indeed sitting pretty. When Malone returned to Quebec and Lalonde was traded off for a raw rookie, fans openly sighed: "Canadiens will never be the same."

When Canadiens were called to training camp for the 1924/25 season, Dandurand had all the regulars, including Sprague and Couture. He had also signed four new players: Sylvio Mantha, Billy Cameron, Bobby Boucher and another "unproven amateur kid," Howie Morenz.

But there was no elation among the Montreal fans. How could the fans, or even Dandurand, have guessed that Canadiens had come up with a superstar who would lift hockeydom from its collective seat and dwarf any superstar the game had ever known up to then?

The Missing No. 7

When Detroit Red Wings' Gordie Howe broke into the NHL, he was only eighteen years old. It was a question as to whether he'd stick, but stick he did—just barely, with seven goals, fifteen assists in fifty-eight Wings games and nothing at all in five playoff games. But he was now a major leaguer and returning to Saskatoon, Saskatchewan, full of anticipation. All the way from Detroit (by train) he had pictured wide-eyed guys and gals with gee-whiz questions about the greats of hockey, whom he had not only seen, but played with and against.

Outside of his family, the first greeting came from an old school buddy on Main Street. "Hi, Gord!" he said, "Where have you been all winter?"

Almost a quarter of a century earlier, there was another rookie destined for superstardom who approached the Big Time without any of Gordie's starry-eyed enthusiasm. In fact, he was homesick and had wept while pleading to be excused from playing for—believe it or not—the Montreal Canadiens. Stubbornly, Canadiens refused to take back the contract and money given the rookie for signing—all $850 of it.

If you're a younger fan, it's likely you have wondered at some time why there is no No. 7 sweater swishing

around the ice with Canadiens. It has been retired by the
club in lasting tribute to that weeping rookie of yesteryear who wore it into hockey immortality—he died following a bone-fracturing crash in all-out NHL action on
the Montreal Forum ice.

Howie Morenz, No. 7

He was an immediate star—one of the very, very few
the National Hockey League has ever known. As I write
this, thirty years after his death in 1937, he is still one
of only eighteen players in the league's half-century
history who has won membership in the ultra-exclusive
250-goal club.

Actually, Howie totalled 270 goals in 546 regular
league games over a span of a little less than fourteen
seasons.

I have often wondered how many goals his free-
wheeling, fast-skating, blasting-shot style would have produced if he had played his career after the redline was
introduced—six seasons after his death.

When he entered the NHL the ice was divided into
three zones with forward passing allowed in the middle
zone. Four seasons after he entered, forward passes were
allowed in the defending and middle zone. The following
season, 1928/29, saw forward passes allowed in all three
zones but a forward pass still had to begin and be completed within a single zone.

The big change—the one made for speedsters of the
Morenz type—came only in 1943/44 with the introduction of the redline across centre ice. This allowed a
forward pass to begin and be completed anywhere within
a team's defending half of the ice—for instance, the
goaler could now whip a long pass all the way up to a
forward on the move at mid-ice. Howie was so fast that
the threat of his breaking away would have held back
attacking defencemen and left the ice much more open
for him to gather pucks and take off.

The redline, throughout his career, could easily have

meant one hundred more goals and matched him with another Canadien great, Jean Beliveau, at the same fourteen-season career point.

That matching, of course, is only on a goals-scored basis. They weren't at all alike in size or style. Morenz was more like the modern-day Bobby Hull in style, speed and shot—in memory's eye I see no difference in size, although I know Morenz weighed only 165 as compared with Hull's 193.

Again, Morenz, like another Canadien immortal to follow—Rocket Richard—tended to challenge the opposing defences by dazzling dash and deception rather than by shooting from longer range and following up for a possible rebound.

It was this very tendency that led to his tragic finale in the Big Time. At the age of thirty-four he was staging a monumental comeback effort on the night of January 28, 1937, against Chicago Black Hawks when, going all-out at the Forum in Montreal, he tried to circle All-Star defenceman Earl Seibert at the St. Catherine Street end of the rink.

Seibert got a piece of him and Howie went flying, skates first, into the boards. The point of one skate imbedded itself in the wood as the rest of Howie rolled over. There was something about the crash that instantly took it out of the realm of the ordinary. I recall how his two line mates, Aurel Joliat and "Black Cat" Johnny Gagnon whipped in, dropping their sticks to kneel beside him, how we of the press as well as the entire crowd rose fearfully to our feet. A profound hush fell on the rink as the players—Canadiens and Hawks intermingled—carried him off.

We didn't know that the next time Howie would be seen out at his beloved centre-ice spot would be in a coffin, with the famous of hockey as pallbearers and with, for the last time, a capacity crowd drawn by the magic of the name.

Three times he had won the Hart (most valuable
player) Trophy, three times he made All-Star teams
although these annual selections began only in the eighth
season of his career. Twice he had won the NHL scoring
championship. But his contribution to major hockey was
vastly greater than any trophies could signify.

His reckless glamour actually sold the game to the
United States—he was, in effect, the "Babe Ruth of
Hockey."

Hockey took some selling below the border, strange
as it may seem to Canadians, for the simple reason that
comparatively few of the potential paying fans had ever
played the game or knew anything about it. But you
didn't have to know anything about hockey to be lifted
from your seat by Morenz—just as you didn't need to
know anything about baseball to be thrilled by a towering
homer off the bat of the Babe.

It was the magic name of Morenz that "sold" Tex
Rickard, legendary New York sports promoter, on NHL
hockey. In fact, Madison Square Garden didn't even have
an ice plant in its building plans until Tex visited Montreal to see Canadiens play and got bitten by the bug—the
Morenz bug.

Until 1925/26 there was only one American team in
the NHL, the Boston Bruins. But it was realized that the
key to expansion lay in New York where Rickard, busy
with blueprints for the new Garden, remained supremely
indifferent to what he regarded a purely Canadian game.

Backstage in the big deal was a Montrealer, Tom
Duggan, who owned two racetracks there and shared
another at Cincinnati with Manhattan's sportsman-boot-
legger, Big Bill Dwyer, then at the peak of his "popularity" in the prohibition era. (A later investigation
revealed that he was so well organized in New York that
the fire department frequently handled rush deliveries to
thirsty bigwigs running short.)

It was Duggan who, after lengthy coaxing, succeeded

in laying on a party that included Rickard and the great sports columnist, Damon Runyon, to visit Montreal and take in a Canadiens game. Rickard couldn't get his eyes off Morenz; hockey took on a new meaning for him. He talked now of including an ice plant at Madison Square Garden. When Duggan pressed about an NHL team, Rickard said he *might* be interested in a team of established NHL calibre, *if* he didn't have to pay for it.

Duggan had the answer. The Hamilton Tigers had finished on top of the league in 1924/25 only to default to Canadiens in the playoffs—the players had gone on strike for a bigger slice of the revenue. Hamilton fans were ripping mad. Duggan rushed to Big Bill Dwyer and got Dwyer to offer seventy-five thousand dollars for the Tigers. The offer was accepted and Rickard had his team —to be known as the New York Americans.

It was significant that the master showman Rickard promptly pressured the NHL president, then Frank Calder, into drafting the 1925/26 schedule so that Canadiens would open the Madison Square Garden hockey season against Americans. Calder was only too glad to allot December 15, 1925 (the thirty-six-game schedule was then only half what it is now).

It was quite a spectacle—Rickard's publicity tub-thumpers had concentrated on the angle that New York's rock-ribbed Americans, formerly the fearsome Tigers of Canada, would be opposing. "Those Flying Frenchmen from Montreal WITH MORENZ."

They would play for a new trophy donated by the Prince of Wales.

The canny promoter also injected a high society note —wooing Manhattan's monied bluebloods by announcing that a generous slice of the proceeds would go to the Neurological Institute of New York. One paper later reported: "Spectacular and thrilling as the match was, the game itself was secondary to the social side of the occasion. Prominent Canadians who had been pouring

into the city for two days, society and city officials, filled
the boxes and arena seats to capacity."

The report continued: "The boxes and arena seats were
resplendent with varied coloured dresses and the black
and white of men's dinner jackets. A number of the
women wore goloshes over their evening slippers. Mayor-
elect Jimmy Walker and Mrs. Walker had a box."

Actually the social list of Who's Who present occupied
one and a half columns of press space in small, eye-strain-
ing 5½-point type. Names such as Choate, Rothschild,
Crowninshield, Carnegie, Barnum and Ringling were
included. Afterwards a supper dance followed at the
Biltmore Hotel with the Canadian Club as hosts and Paul
Whiteman's orchestra providing dance music. The players
of both teams were honoured guests.

The game?

An eight-column headline in the New York *Times* the
next day read: BRILLIANT GATHERING OF 17,000 PER-
SONS AT FORMAL OPENING OF GARDEN.

The story went on:

From the land of ice and snow there came to New York
last night a new game to celebrate the formal opening
of Madison Square Garden . . . in the tiers of flag-draped
boxes was a social registered representation which was
something entirely new in New York's long history of the
events of sport . . . . No sport in any man's town ever got
the rousing greeting that Canada's great game got in
Rickard's new amphitheatre . . . . This was no common
or garden variety of sporting event. It assumed the importance of a momentous Event with a capital E. Much
water will flow under the Brooklyn Bridge before New
York witnesses a sporting carnival with so much fuss and
ostentation as that which attended the introduction of
pro hockey in Gotham . . . . The Lobby looked like the
foyer of the opera . . . furs, jewels, flashes of cerise, Nile
greens . . . .

The Canadiens paraded around the ice behind the Governor-General's Foot Guards band (ablaze in red coats, gold braid and great shakos). The Americans skated behind the military band from West Point (with its trim blue uniforms, the white-lined capes thrown back over their shoulders).

Immediately before the game's start, the two great bands faced one another across the rink. With a roof-raising deep-booming of brass horns supplemented by cornets, bugles and trombones, the Foot Guards played "God Save the King." Then the West Point band, supplemented by the Academy's Bugle and Drum Corps, gave with a rousing "Star-Spangled Banner."

Americans' captain, Billy Burch, and Morenz scrambled at the face-off and Big Time hockey was under way in the new Garden. Americans' left winger Shorty Green stole the show with an early goal but a deep groan followed as referee Cooper Smeaton, now trustee of the Stanley Cup, called it back on an offside ruling. But Shorty couldn't be stopped and, to the thunderous glee of the assembled thousands, scored the very first goal on Garden ice at 11.55 of the first period. Canadiens went ahead in the second period on goals by Battleship Leduc and Billy Boucher. The 3-1 insurance goal was bagged in the third period by Howie Morenz on a rebound from a sizzling shot by Aurel Joliat.

The *Times* reporter, Harry Cross, was apparently left in awe of the checking—"at times vigorously rough." The play he found "fast and furious." His overall conclusion was that the game "is sure to gain popularity."

While the "fast and slippery" ability of Joliat apparently keyed the Canadien win, it was apparent that the reckless speed spurts of Morenz caught popular fancy.

I have often been faced with the curious problem of explaining the magic of Morenz to modern fans. The simplest way, possibly, is to compare him with the modern-day great, Bobby Hull. But that isn't quite enough. Only recently, a wing mate of Morenz's towards the latter's finale with Canadiens, the one and only "Black Cat" Johnny Gagnon, added to that comparison: "Like Hull to a degree; whereas Hull is inclined to do some circling inside the opposing blueline, Morenz always went straight and headlong for the defence." But even that doesn't seem to satisfy those who wonder why he has been placed in the upper stratum of superstars.

For instance, a few years ago I visited the home of Bernard (Boom Boom) Geoffrion, himself a former Canadien superstar and the NHL sensation of 1966/67 by virtue of a thrilling comeback with New York Rangers at the age of thirty-six. His beautiful wife, Marlene, asked me during the course of the evening:

"Just how good was my Dad?"

Marlene, daughter of the late Howie, was a child when he died. "Boom Boom" had never seen him play.

Just recently a thirty-four-year-old radio broadcaster asked me: "Was Howie Morenz actually as great as the stars we have seen or are seeing today?"

The question, as it always does, stopped me for a moment until I realized the broadcaster had been only four years old when Howie died. The answer can, I know, sound strained because storybook goals often sound alike in the telling—in the telling most greats are a blending of fast skater, tricky stick-handler and hard shooter.

Just how can one explain to a thirty-year-old fan the "different" magic of a star thirty years dead? Could Morenz really have been as good as the modern-day greats they know?

My own descriptions never seem adequate so I revert to two descriptions of goals he scored, one as told by a fellow sports writer, Baz O'Meara, and the other by Howie's left-wing line mate, Aurel Joliat. The mental pictures created by those two descriptions tell of the "something special" about Howie.

Baz, now with the Montreal *Star,* was covering a game in Ottawa in 1930 when Canadiens were playing Ottawa Senators—then in the NHL.

The Senators were leading, 4-2; they looked unbeatable especially since Morenz had gone into the game with a bad ankle and had shown only briefly—and ineffectively. With six minutes to go there came a stop in play and Morenz asked coach Cecil Hart to send him on.

Hart hesitated. Should he risk aggravating his top star's injury in an apparently hopeless cause? Should he . . . whether or not he had made some slight motion that seemed to indicate approval, or whether or not Morenz simply exploded from the bench under his own tension was never quite certain. Before anything could be done about it, play was resumed and Morenz had the puck . . . under a full head of steam!

Morenz aimed directly for the middle of the Ottawa defence as he so often did—either to go tumbling head first as they "sandwiched" him or to vault through the narrowing opening, pushing aside shoulders, elbows and sticks to land on his skates with the puck and only a frenzied goaler to beat.

But this time Morenz passed at the last split-second before hitting the defence. The puck landed squarely on the stick of Aurel Joliat who bulleted it into the Ottawa net.

Canadiens were back in the hunt, down only 4-3, with a bit more than five minutes to go. Baz O'Meara tells the rest of it.

"Canadiens swarmed to the attack, and the puck spun loose as Alex Smith of Ottawa batted it to the blueline and raced after it fully twenty feet ahead of the nearest Canadien, who was Morenz.

"Flashing on his skates, his bad ankle forgotten, Howie cut down the twenty feet to ten as Smith hit the defence zone. Then fairly hurling himself forward on his skates

Howie reached ahead to tip Smith's stick just as the latter shot.

"The puck went wide, behind the net. Howie kept his momentum and circled the net in a blurring flash, passing Smith before the amazed Ottawa star had a chance to set himself for the return rush.

"Morenz was now a meteor—the full length of the ice, through the disorganized Ottawa defence alignment which was now watching Joliat, in on goal and finishing with a blasting shot that could have torn the head off a sphinx. Score: Ottawa 4; Canadiens 4.

"The game went into overtime. Morenz was all over the ice. You could sense what was coming—and it did. Morenz broke up the game with the 5-4 goal. The hostile crowd broke into a storm of cheers—for years Ottawa talked about that game Morenz had played. When he died, the hockey-wise town recalled it anew as evidence of the great heart and boyish love of hockey that burned therein."

The other description of Morenz in action, the on-ice version of his dashing line mate, Aurel Joliat, concerned what he called "Howie's goal of goals."

I will never quite forget Aurel's dramatic description as he told me one night in 1962 at an information wicket in the Union Station at Ottawa where Aurel, then sixty years old, was employed. His unconcealed hero-worship of his late team mate made it hard to realize that he, too, had been a superstar. In the Hockey Hall of Fame, this astonishing mite who forced speed, cunning and dogged determination to compensate for a meagre one hundred and forty pounds is credited with the same number of goals, two hundred and seventy, as is Howie. "The Little Giant," it is true, took sixteen seasons to amass that total but he was voted to four All-Star teams, won the Hart Trophy once and helped Canadiens to three Stanley Cup victories.

The "goal of goals" was understandably easy to pin-

point in history—it won the 1931 Stanley Cup for
Canadiens.

The semi-finals had been gruelling with Boston extending the series to the then five-game limit—three of
the games going into overtime. The final series, against
Chicago, proved a continuation of the grind; two of the
best-of-five games had gone into overtime. Now, in the
fifth game, as Joliat saw it:

"Morenz had rushed away from us with the puck down
centre and was checked at the Chicago defence. Some
Chicago forward picked up the loose puck at the gallop
but I checked him at mid-ice.

"I had taken only two strides when I heard 'Joliat!'
screamed at me from right wing. It was incredible; even
with the play going at top speed Morenz had raced back
on my left wing, whirled around behind me and had
again picked up full speed down right wing.

"To catch him before he went offside at the blueline
I had to fire a shot rather than a pass. Howie picked up
the puck as if he was using a lacrosse stick and without
losing a stride.

"He was by the Chicago defence in a flash and in on
goalie Chuck Gardiner before anybody really recognized
the menace. His shot, fired with every last ounce from
an exhausted body, hit an upper corner of the net. The
Forum crowd gasped then raised the roof in one ear-
splitting wave of cheering thunder. That had to be
Howie's finest goal."

Such was the Morenz electricity that shocked the new
rinks of the United States into tingling awareness of a
pulsating, "imported" sport. It also was the American
relaunching of a tradition already launched on Canadian
rinks—the speed-crazy, win-hungry tradition of Les
Canadiens hockey.

This was the same Morenz who had wept on being told
he had to be a Canadien.

Born in Mitchell, Ontario, Howie moved as a child

with his parents to Stratford. By the time he was four-teen Howie was showing considerable promise with the town's junior team that won the Ontario Hockey Association title. He kept improving in intermediate hockey but, for some reason I have never been able to determine, the scouts of the nearby NHL Toronto St. Pats (later Maple Leafs) were not excited about him.

Actually, Leo Dandurand, then bossman of Montreal Canadiens, told me he first heard of the "kid" in 1923. The kid was then twenty years old!

A former Canadien player, Ernie Suave, returned from refereeing a game in Stratford and told Dandurand about "a kid named Morenz who scored so many goals they had to yank him."

Dandurand didn't treat the report too seriously—after all, if the player was that good wouldn't Toronto have him already tied up? It was some weeks later that Dandurand asked Lou Marsh, then refereeing as well as writing sports for the Toronto *Daily Star,* about Morenz. Marsh had never heard of him but promised to take a look on his next trip to Stratford.

More time passed before a letter arrived from Marsh —raving about Morenz and urging action.

Dandurand sent a former Wanderer goalie, Riley Hern, to Stratford with a twenty-five-hundred-dollar contract. Hern, obviously surprised, reported back to Dandurand that young Morenz wasn't interested. He had a job in Stratford, loved his intermediate hockey team and didn't want to leave. Dandurand, now at the close of the Canadiens' 1922/23 season and anxious to wrap up things before taking off for his racing interests in the American Midwest, said to forget the whole thing.

In July, a long distance call from Marsh again urged Dandurand to act because the Toronto team was "warming up" on Morenz. Marsh suggested a cash offer because the lad had some small debts to clean up in Stratford.

Thus was born what had to be the all-time bargain

deal of National Hockey League history. Dandurand
sent Cecil Hart, later the great Canadien coach, to Stratford with a heap of small bills.

Although totalling only $850, it was quite a heap as
seen in those days on a living room table in Stratford,
Ontario. Howie nodded in wide-eyed agreement and his
equally excited father signed for him—Howie wasn't
yet of age.

The quiet summer erupted into wintry war. The citi-
zens of Toronto raged over the "kidnapping" of a player
from the St. Pats area by the Montreal team. Howie was
aghast at the abuse heaped on him by his own Stratford
fans for "deserting" Ontario. A local minister organized
a campaign against the ruthless representatives of "sinful
Montreal" for wooing a fine, under-aged boy away from
his home life into the world of crass professionalism.

On August tenth, Dandurand received a letter to which
was attached a certified cheque for $850. It was from
Howie Morenz who apologized for the expense and in-
convenience caused but, for reasons of family and work,
he begged for the return of the contract.

Dandurand saw nothing heart-rending in the letter;
what he saw was a plot by the Toronto team to get
Howie. Dandurand raged to the press: "If Morenz
doesn't play for us he'll play pro hockey nowhere else."

Dandurand's big ace-up-sleeve, however, was some
private information he had obtained that Howie was
getting eight hundred dollars a season "under the table"
to play in Stratford. Dandurand quietly let it be known
in OHA executive circles that he planned to "blow the lid
off amateur hockey in Ontario" if Morenz wasn't persuaded to honour his contract.

Howie made the trip to Montreal. Before a stern Dandurand he pleaded for release; he wasn't happy, his town
wasn't happy, his parents weren't happy. He broke down
and cried.

Dandurand's steely front melted. He decided on another approach. They would have lunch and resume their talk later.

A rush call was sent to all available Canadiens to rush by taxi to one of Montreal's most lavish restaurants where they sat around a large table. Young Morenz, pop-eyed amid so many headline NHL figures, sat through the luncheon in a state of excited daze as everybody made a fuss over him. An afternoon of relaxed pleasure followed by dinner at Dandurand's posh home followed. Howie was escorted in strength to the railway station that night.

"Report to our training camp at Grimsby, Ontario," Dandurand told Howie, "and if you're unhappy after two weeks we'll have another talk."

Howie reported, but in the first week a deluge of long distance phone calls from Stratford fans left him near tears again. On Saturday he asked to go home for the weekend. Dandurand hired a car, told Howie to forget about the scheduled practice on Sunday and sent Howie home with an escort who was ordered to bring Howie back for Monday practice, bound and gagged if necessary.

Howie came back for Monday but he was unhappier than ever. He remained that way right up to the opening night of the season—in Toronto, of all places.

The publicity had jammed the rink—in addition to angry Toronto fans, half the town of Stratford had made the trip. The Stratford delegation was torn between two loyalties—as Ontario rooters they sided with Toronto but, again, Howie was their boy.

The game played on December fifteenth at the Toronto Arena saw the Toronto St. Pats win, 2-1, before a packed house. But the local as well as visiting press agreed that "rookie Morenz was the fastest man on the ice."

He was in on the lone Canadien goal, scored by line

mate Aurel Joliat. He got through on Toronto goalie
John Ross Roach several times but big saves kept him
off the scoring sheet. Only one intriguing criticism was
noted: "He wastes too much energy on needless skating
—coach Leo Dandurand should be able to teach him to
conserve it."

Nobody ever did teach him—that was Morenz.

The feel of the Big Time, the realization that he'd
never be happy facing a weaker challenge got Howie that
night. He never looked back.

His first goal came on the night of December twenty-
sixth; it had a typical Canadian flare for the historic. That
night marked the opening of the new Ottawa Auditorium. The rock-ribbed Senators "handed it out to
Morenz right and left but the Stratford kid, playing a
whale of a game, made his scoring debut."

Howie's singing skates sparked Canadiens that season
to their first Stanley Cup in the seven-year history of the
NHL. In a two-game, total-goals Eastern playoff against
Ottawa, Canadiens won, 5-2, with Morenz netting three
and assisting on the fourth.

In the Stanley Cup semi-finals against Vancouver and
the finals against Calgary, Canadiens made it a four-
game sweep in which Howie scored four goals and
assisted on a fifth. In those same four games, the Canadiens totalled fourteen goals—the line with Morenz at
centre, flanked by Joliat and Billy Boucher, accounted
for twelve of them. The line's average weight was one
hundred and forty pounds.

Howie soared to his goal-scoring peak in 1929/30;
with the NHL playing a forty-four game schedule he
notched forty goals and assisted on ten. Twice he won
the NHL scoring championship. Three times he was
awarded the Hart (most valuable player to his team)
Trophy.

What kind of fellow was Howie Morenz at his peak?
I knew him in the dressing room where he was idolized.

I saw him, always fashionably dressed and laughingly
alert, winding his way through crowds of autograph-
hunting kids and adults in the Forum hallways and on
the street. I had occasion to do a feature on him at his
home and recall my photographer's difficulties—his three
youngsters, Howie junior, Marlene and Donald insisted
on rough-housing all over him as we tried for a more or
less dignified shot.

I was hoping the father would restore order but he
never raised his voice—this hardened athlete of major
hockey confessed: "I just can't scold them—they seem to
get a hurt look in their eyes that kills me."

There was another side to him that was described by
Elmer Ferguson, then sports editor of the Montreal
Herald (now dean of sports writers with the *Star*), in a
column on March 9, 1937—the day after Howie died:

"There was a night in Boston in 1929. Canadiens, then
at or near the peak of their all-time greatness, battled
the powerful Boston machine of that era in a pair of
gripping matches, losing both by 1-0 scores.

"I was sleeping soundly when at six o'clock in the
morning after the second game, there was a knock on
my door. It was Morenz, face still drawn from the toll of
fierce, close conflict the night before. He was dressed for
the street. But he wasn't going out. He had just come in.

"He had tramped the winding, crooked streets of
Boston all night, his mind still in a raging torrent of
turmoil and conflict, through which the episodes of the
battle were running. 'I couldn't sleep,' he apologized,
'now I want to talk.' "

"And so we talked, far on towards noon. Play after
play he ran through, analyzed, putting a finger on the
spot where a different stride, another shift, might have
meant the whole tide of battle. . . . Other players had long
since dismissed defeat and the game from their minds
and were sleeping peacefully, but not Morenz. He
blamed only himself for the team's defeats."

Ferguson recalled another night, in Ottawa, when the home team's Hec Kilrea, in a moment of impulse, swung his stick heavily and hit Morenz on the head, knocking him out. Morenz recovered consciousness only in the dressing room and his first words were:

"I bet Hec didn't mean that. He's a good guy."

Incredibly, Montreal turned on Morenz eleven seasons after he joined the Canadiens. It is a razor-keen hockey city but a harsh one. Its fans refused to see fading legs and saw only fading desire as the fierce energy began burning out of the thirty-two-year-old Howie.

Manager Leo Dandurand levelled blistering attacks on the fans. It was no use. To restore Howie's badly hurt pride, Dandurand accepted the eager offer from Chicago Black Hawks and sold him to the American team for 1934/35.

Howie followed orders and concentrated on a play-making role but his heart wasn't in Chicago and part way through 1935/36, he was traded to New York Rangers for Glenn Brydson.

It was just what Howie needed. New York hailed him as a star of stars, the staid *Times* ran a heading: "Here Comes Howie!" The press revived the feats of the "Swift Swiss" (he was actually of Swiss descent and never managed to learn a word of French).

New York's welcome came on January 28, 1936, when he donned the Ranger colours. Exactly one year later, on the same date, he suffered his tragic accident wearing a Canadien sweater. In the summer, Cecil Hart, offered the pilot post with Canadiens, agreed only on condition that the team "bring back Morenz to where he belongs".

The Canadiens did and the fickle fans greeted him with the welcome of a returning hero. Happy again, Howie tried to reclimb the heights of his great moments. It was during such a Big Try that he crashed into the boards and suffered a double fracture. He was taken to Hôpital Saint-Luc, suffering intense agony.

In those days there were no NHL games played on Sunday nights so visiting teams at the Montreal Forum on Saturdays didn't leave until the next day. Such was the esteem in which Howie was held that his friendly foes invariably visited him around midnight on Saturdays bringing along generous quantities of festive cheer.

Hindsight makes us all experts. Perhaps the hospital authorities should have been tougher about visiting hours but certainly it must have been difficult to foresee anything in the nature of a cardiac failure in such a symbol of the dynamic athlete. From out of the blue the news stunned an unbelieving Montreal on March 8, 1937:

"Howie Morenz is dead!"

The impact on the Canadian metropolis was matched in my experience only with the flash about President John Kennedy's assassination. Both Morenz and Kennedy had carried such a popular image of vigour and vibrant life that death seemed just too shockingly unthinkable.

Howie Morenz's body lay in state at mid-ice in the Forum, exactly where he had faced off so many hundreds of times. Hockey's greats took turns as guard of honour around the bier, day and night.

The afternoon of the funeral service I reached the Forum a little late. So great was the crowd jamming the front doors on St. Catherine Street that I went around to the side entrance on Closse Street. It, too, was jammed. I finally got in through the boiler-room entrance. As I emerged from the lower reaches of the famed rink into a hallway I recall how the profound silence surprised me —had they locked the doors against the fans and decided to hold the service in an empty building?

Then I found myself on the lower promenade. My breath was taken away. There were some fifteen thousand fans, normally the noisiest in hockeydom, seated in absolute silence with heads bowed. Reverend

Malcolm Campbell had spoken of life that ended too soon but left an undying memory. The minister concluded with the lines:

> The heights by great men reached and kept,
> Were not achieved by sudden flight,
> But they while their companions slept,
> Were toiling upward in the night.

It was a blistering cold, sub-zero day but some two hundred thousand Montrealers lined the streets as the cortege passed en route to Mount Royal Cemetery in the second-to-last tribute honouring the player who had either scored or assisted in scoring four hundred and ninety goals in less than fourteen seasons.

The final tribute was paid eight months later at the Forum when the stars of the NHL played the Morenz Memorial Game with all proceeds going to Howie's family. The official programme carried a full page advertisement dedicated "To the Memory of a Great Athlete" and containing a dedication by an unnamed author that impressed itself indelibly on my mind:

Superb skill, sublime courage and sincere modesty were his and wherever hockey is played, now or ever—Howie Morenz will be recalled as the "beau sabreur" of hockey —Sans peur, Sans reproche.

The Era Explosive

*Normally, a tie-game doesn't leave anybody excited.
When it does leave fifteen thousand Toronto fans not
only excited but electrified over the dazzling display of
their Pet Hate No. 1 with invading Montreal Canadiens,
it has to be a deadlock that is far from dead.*

*In the 4-4 game of February 15, 1947, Rocket
Richard turned the Maple Leaf Gardens on end as he
scored three picture-play goals and assisted on the other.
The four points increased his lead in the NHL scoring
race at that stage to nine points.*

Red Burnett of the Toronto Daily Star *pushed his way
into the Canadiens' dressing-room with a photographer.
Red asked Richard to kiss his hat-trick-scoring stick for
a photo.*

*"Kiss it yourself!" snapped the Rocket, "we didn't win,
did we?"*

Le Club de Hockey Canadien Inc. was bleakly minding
its own business when the Era Explosive burst upon it in
the 1943/44 season. The team hadn't finished higher
than fourth in five seasons; they hadn't survived the playoff semi-finals for a dozen years. Canadiens weren't really
bothering anybody but everybody was bothering them.

The explosive force that flared Canadiens from the

serenity of the chronic also-ran category into the stratosphere of world champion was an unlikely addition of
the previous season from the Canadiens' senior amateur
team. His formal name, Joseph Henri Maurice Richard,
was eventually shortened to "Rocket" Richard (by the
now sports editor of the Montreal *Star*, Hal Atkins)
for obvious reasons.

I say "unlikely" and that's exactly what Richard was
—incredible as hindsight makes that appear. Much later
he himself mused as we sat together in a train bound for
somewhere:

"I can't figure what Canadiens saw in me to offer that
first pro contract. It seemed I was always on my ass or in
the hospital."

In his very first game with the senior amateur club
he had broken his left ankle and was out for the season.
In the middle of the next season he broke a wrist and was
on the shelf again. In two seasons as a senior he had
played only twenty-two games, yet the NHL Canadiens
brought him up for 1942/43. In his sixteenth NHL
game, he broke the other ankle.

Coach Dick Irvin said aloud what even the hospital-
haunting, twenty-one-year-old rookie was already thinking: "I doubt if Richard is going to make it; this league is
just too tough for him."

Canadiens actually offered Richard to New York
Rangers as a trade for Phil Watson but the late Lester
Patrick, then Ranger ruler, scornfully dismissed the
suggestion. What might have the trade done for the
Rangers? It's natural to conclude that Richard would
have changed the Ranger destiny just as he changed
Canadiens' but I'm not at all sure that Richard would
have soared to the same heights as a Ranger, for a reason
that was part luck and part coaching genius.

The luck came from his luckless ankles; with his
history, the Army wanted no part of Maurice Richard
and a wartime shortage of talent was being felt. There

had been nothing to indicate extraordinary pro promise in his kid hockey at St. Francois de Laval School or at Montreal Tech, or even later in juvenile league action on Park Lafontaine's public rinks. Injuries bugged him in junior hockey with Verdun and, while it was true that he was moved up to senior with a year of junior eligibility still left, the wartime shortage was a more potent factor; although coach Dave Campbell of the seniors does deserve full marks for seeing enough in the teenager to make the early move.

Campbell was one of three coaches who deserve credit under the heading, "coaching genius," when we consider the beginning of stardom for Maurice Richard.

The second, and key one, was Paul Haynes who was coaching the Canadiens' seniors during the twenty-one games in which Richard played in that second season. Haynes, now a prominent Montreal business executive, had a ten-season NHL playing background (Montreal Maroons, Boston Bruins and the Canadiens) as well as a remarkable scouting record for Canadiens. On the same trip he had hit the jackpot by coming up with two present members of hockey's Hall of Fame, Elmer Lach and Kenny Reardon. Lach, it isn't widely known even today, had already been to the Toronto training camp twice and, at one time, had been on the Rangers' list.

Haynes noticed something in a practice session— something that made left-winger Maurice Richard a bit unusual. Normally, a player coming in on that wing has the choice of either trying to veer around the left side of the defence or shoot. If neither course is practicable the alternative (if no passing play is feasible) is to cut into the heavy traffic in front of the defence and try for a backhand shot.

"However, I noticed that Richard had developed a trick brand new in my experience," Haynes told me. "He had a hard backhander which kept the defence 'honest' when he had to cut over from left wing to his 'wrong' side. But he used the threat of the backhander more as a decoy. In a flash he would switch around the defenceman over on his right-wing side, using the sheer strength of his left arm to buttonhook by his opponent while bringing the puck around for a prime-position shot on the goaler. Whereas the right wingers shoot from their right side, Maurice came in shooting from his left side. In other words, instead of shooting from an angle, he was shooting from almost dead centre."

Haynes hastened to add: "Don't go suggesting that all kids should play opposite their natural shooting side —if ninety out of one hundred good players tried that trick they'd get creamed by the other defenceman in the narrow passage left between defence and goal crease. But Maurice had an extraordinary surge of speed combined with extraordinary shoulder strength."

Haynes recognized the danger of the play. Like all plays in all sports, they don't always work and when Maurice's buttonhooking was a bit slow he was open for crushing bodychecks while off-balance from the other defenceman. This was the cause of many of his injuries.

Tommy Gorman, general manager of the Forum, and coach Dick Irvin deliberated for a long time before deciding to offer Richard a contract. Both saw him as fragile, but also saw something spectacular in the apparently awkward style. Irvin always liked players who skated with their feet wide apart and showed a desire for shooting only when the whites of the goaler's eyes were visible. Gorman was inclined to overlook some defects for the benefit of getting another French name on the roster. Besides it wouldn't take much to coax a twenty-dollar-a-week CPR machinist out of the shops.

So it was decided to take on Richard—but only as a left winger. Canadiens were solid on the right-wing side with Gordie Drillon, Joe Benoit and ill-fated Tony Demers, possessor of a big shot and an off-ice proneness to big trouble.

Richard signed on October 29, 1942, and his first
NHL game was on a line with Lach at centre and Demers
at right wing. The line's debut was an almost instant success, producing a goal against Boston Bruins in thirty-six
seconds. Demers scored, with Lach and Richard getting
assists. Richard's first NHL goal was a solo effort on the
night of November 8, 1942, against the Rangers. The
goaler was somebody named Steve Buzinski—if that goal
was the cause of his leaving the scene early, it must be
of some comfort now to realize that other NHL goalers
fanned on a total of 625 other Richard goals.

Richard was still playing on left wing on December
twenty-seventh, when he tried to buttonhook around
Bruin defenceman Johnny Crawford, was hit heavily and
crashed into the boards where his right ankle snapped.
That ended his first NHL season; but five goals and six
assists in sixteen games warranted a tryout ticket to the
1943/44 training camp.

In the course of experimenting with various combina-
nations, Dick Irvin (the third and decisive figure under
the "coaching genius" heading in the career-shaping of
Richard) put Richard on a line with Lach and "Toe"
Blake. They were all left-handed shots but Irvin, recalling that Richard had impressed Haynes on the "wrong"
side, assigned to right wing this one-hundred-and-seventy-
five-pounder with eager ways and flashing eyes atop a
five-foot-ten frame.

Irvin soon noted something that sold him. In playing
the right alley permanently, Richard had more chance to
test his buttonhook technique and, even when a defenceman would ride him off, Richard's sizzling backhander
was a double-threat shot. Goalers find backhanders
harder to judge than shots from a shooter's normal side,
but Richard added to that difficulty by firing while
blocked from the goaler's vision by the defenceman's
body. A wrist shot snapped by powerful wrists with a

Agony and the ecstasy of Canadiens' general manager, Sammy
Pollock, reflects that being "brass" doesn't eliminate fan fever.
White-haired man seated ahead of him in this sequence is
Cooper Smeaton, trustee of the Stanley Cup.

Toe Blake reflected back-of-the-bench strain leading up to his
retirement in 1969 after setting the record for coaching Stanley
Cup winning teams: eight (all Canadiens teams).

Coach Toe Blake in champagne mood after winning seventh
Stanley Cup (1966) as coach of Canadiens.

Chicago Goalie Glenn Hall (L) congratulates Canadien goalie
Gump Worsley after Canadiens' Stanley Cup win in 1965.

Coach Blake and team, 1966.

Canadiens' Frank Mahovlich (L) is beaten to the puck by
Boston Bruins' fabulous Bobby Orr during the 1971 playoffs
resulting in upset defeat for the Bruins. The Big M ended top
playoff scorer.

Payment to Canada Wide Syndicate

Weekend Magazine
Photo by Frank Prazak

Ken Dryden, Canadiens' miracle man of the nets in the 1971
playoffs, holds the Conn Smythe Trophy awarded the outstanding player in the playoffs.

The embattled Canadiens' coaches of 1970-71. After Claude Ruel (R) quit during the season, assistant Al MacNeil took over and ran into open rebellion while in the playoffs.

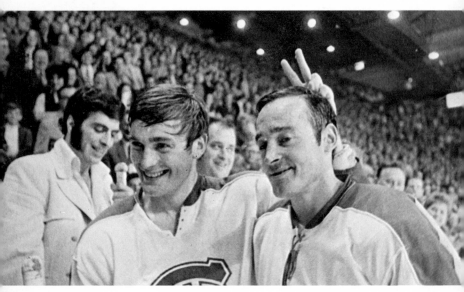

Jubilant Pete Mahovlich gives the V-for-Victory sign over the back of brother Frank's head at the Forum after 4-3 Canadiens' win in game No. 6 of 1971 Stanley Cup finals against Chicago. Frank set up Pete for the winning goal.

minimum of warning, in close, can be as tough to judge
and handle as any slap shot.

Thus was born Canadiens' fabulous Punch Line.

And from the Punch Line, the Rocket took off to
breathtaking heights. Canadiens made a shambles of the
regular (at that time) fifty-game schedule, losing only
five games. Richard played in forty-six of them, scored
thirty-six goals and went on to shatter a playoff record
with twelve goals in nine games. In one of the playoffs,
a semi-final against Toronto, he staged the greatest one-
man display in NHL playoff history by scoring all five
goals as Canadiens won, 5-1. The three-star selection on
the Imperial Oil broadcast blared:

"Richard, Richard . . . and Richard!"

Canadiens scored thirty-nine goals in the nine playoff
games; the Punch Line accounted for twenty-one of
them. The final four of those twenty-one made up a
hockey story that no self-respecting fiction writer would
consider believable enough to use.

The scene was the Forum on the night of April thirteenth. It was the fourth game of the final series, against
Chicago Black Hawks. Canadiens had won the first three
and went into this game heavy favourites with the betting
fraternity.

But the team went sour. With ten minutes to go Canadiens were trailing 4-1, and the Hawks shifted into a
tightly defensive game. Somebody, likely some frustrated
fan who had wagered a four-straight, started a chant:

"Fake! Fake! Fake!"

Other fans who were just plain bored took up the
chant for kicks. Down on the ice the message finally got
to the Punch Line and they came to life with the most
awesome display of sheer hockey fight I have ever seen
on a National Hockey League rink.

Elmer Lach, one hundred and seventy pounds of go-
and-guts from Saskatchewan way, made it 4-2 with a

shot from ten feet out that could have decapitated goalie Mike Karakas if the puck hadn't missed his head.

With five minutes to go, the Rocket left the launching pad and backhanded the 4-3 counter. The crowd hadn't a chance to resume its collective seat before Toe Blake bulleted a pass out from behind the Chicago net that the Rocket met with a savage slapshot . . . the game was tied!

At 9:12 of overtime, Blake scored the Cup-winner. The town was hoarse for three days.

Rocket's eighteen seasons with Canadiens were rip-roaring and rabble-rousing. In 1,111 regular and playoff games he amassed 626 goals, 465 assists. He rewrote the record book; on retiring his name appeared in sixteen records.

He starred with eight Stanley Cup teams. He made either first or second All-Star teams in fourteen of his eighteen seasons. He scored twenty or more goals in fourteen consecutive seasons.

Maker of records. Maker of riots. Nobody was neutral in their opinion of the Rocket during that most fantastic era of Canadiens' history; to the fans he was either the worst thing that ever happened to the National Hockey League, or the best. He was hated intensely, he was loved fanatically. But, on one point all had to agree: there has never been—perhaps never will be—a player to equal him under intense pressure. He was consumed with a ferocity for winning that rose to frenzied peaks, peaks that blended supreme hockey skills and thrills with moments of volcanic turmoil, inexcusably beyond the code of amateur sportsmanship but somehow acceptable in the code of the professional. People who pay their costly way into pro games like sportsmanship but only served as a side dish; the main course for their feast has to be the sense of players going all-out to win. If temper and turmoil erupt in the white-heat of all-out competition it is accepted by the pro crowd as evidence of burning desire by the players to give their money's worth.

Certainly, none of the fifteen million fans who paid to see Richard play failed to get value for money invested. And, perhaps it was the greatest tribute of all, on the night of March 17, 1955, when his suspension-enforced absence was indirectly responsible for forfeiting a game at the end of the first period, only some one hundred of fifteen thousand fans accepted the Forum management's invitation to pick up refunds for their tickets.

The build-up to what has become known in hockey history as The Richard Riot (although he wasn't playing that night) had extended back over a period of fourteen months and reflected the extraordinary ability Rocket seemed to have acquired in either wooing or warring with entire cities.

Rocket's name had been appearing for some time atop a breezy, ghost-written sports column in the French-language Montreal weekly, *Samedi-Dimanche,* under the heading, *Le Tour du Chapeau.* It had first broken into national attention when he became incensed over Quebec City's treatment of brother Henri in a junior game there. Rocket had classed the fans as "bandits" and brought heated demands for an apology from the floor of the Provincial Legislature. The demand, and what caused the demand, were officially ignored by the National Hockey League office but a Rocket-by-lined column of January, 1954, just couldn't be ignored.

There had been a bloody, stick-swinging duel at Madison Square Garden between Rocket's team mate, Boom Boom Geoffrion, and Rangers' Ron Murphy. NHL President Clarence Campbell suspended Geoffrion for "eight New York games" and Murphy, who had suffered a broken jaw, was suspended from five games.

Le Tour du Chapeau pulled no punches and invented a few new ones. Among other things Campbell was charged with creating publicity for himself at the expense "of a good fellow like Boom Boom Geoffrion just because he is a French Canadian."

It was charged that Campbell openly displayed partiality at Forum games by smiling when Canadiens were scored against. That he had failed to fine or suspend either Billy Mosienko of Chicago or Jack Evans of Rangers when those two players had "deliberately" injured Canadiens' Jean Beliveau on two occasions. Nor was Gordie Howe suspended "when he almost knocked out Dollard St. Laurent's eye two years ago."

For good measure, Rocket's column took a sideswipe at Campbell for "paper assists" given Detroit players at home: "It is not surprising that Howe, Lindsay and Reibel are among the top point-scorers in the league." (It should be noted that at this time the Rocket was aiming in no uncertain fashion for the one prize award that had hitherto eluded him, the NHL scoring championship and the thousand dollars going with it.)

The column finished off with a flat challenge to Campbell—if he was punished for the above writing Rocket claimed he would leave hockey "and I have an idea that several other Canadien players who share my opinion will do the same."

Campbell, the ex-army colonel, hailed the column with a twenty-one gun salute—all guns firing point-blank at the Rocket.

The Rocket was shot down in flames after Campbell hauled Selke and vice-president Kenny Reardon on the carpet and ordered them to take disciplinary or corrective action or the NHL would.

The next column in *Samedi-Dimanche* was in the form of a "farewell as a sportswriter" to his readers because "freedom of speech has been taken away from me." A separate editorial was headed, "Richard is Gagged."

The next day Montreal was aghast at a formal announcement by the Canadiens in which Richard "humbly and sincerely" apologized to President Campbell: "The accusations made by me were unfounded and I am anxious that Mr. Campbell's integrity and the honesty of the game be established beyond question".

Richard stated that he was working under "advice" from his club "but no pressure has been placed upon me by either the club or the league."

Furthermore, following advice received, he deposited a personal cheque for one thousand dollars "as evidence of good faith." Should he fail to keep his promise of good faith, he knew the money would be lost but he trusted that otherwise it would be returned "when I finish as a player."

Campbell's terse comment was. "This bond will have no bearing on any trouble the Rocket may get into on the ice".

It was just as well—there was more ice-trouble ahead for the Rocket than even his imaginative ghost-writer could have anticipated.

Montreal fans, accustomed to their Richard the Lion-Hearted, were openly shocked at his lamb-like retreat and even a benign *Amende honorable* editorial in the Montreal *Star* suggesting that the incident should drop from the forefront of attention, failed to ease the sting of shock. An anti-Campbell fan reaction was reaching the boiling point.

Richard ended that season of The Abject Apology second in scoring although he had scored the most goals, thirty-seven. Howe beat him out by virtue of eighteen more assists. Montreal fans spoke sarcastically of "paper assists" in Detroit as mentioned by Richard— although his apology had called the charge "unfounded."

After a long, hot summer spent largely in shrugging off angry fan queries, the Rocket roared into the 1954/55 season at the age of thirty-three like a ferocious rookie.

We all sensed that something would have to blow but nobody imagined that the peak of the Era Explosive was yet to be scaled.

Right in the heart of the goodwill-to-men, Happy-New-Year period of Yuletide jazz on December twenty-ninth at Toronto, Rocket got into a rhubarb with Leafs' Bob Bailey, six feet and one hundred and ninety-seven pounds. When six-foot, two-hundred-pound linesman George Hayes tried to halt the festivities, Rocket whipped him across the chops with an empty glove.

Fully incensed, the Rocket took a lot of calming down —in this case, two misconduct penalties by referee Red Storey. These called for automatic fines of twenty-five dollars apiece. To the fifty dollars, Campbell added two hundred dollars for "gross misconduct" and general flouting of the authority of officials.

This two-hundred-and-fifty-dollar assault on his wallet created another Richard record. It brought his career fines' total up to twenty-five hundred dollars, not including the thousand-dollar bond he had posted to keep the peace . . . off the ice.

The costly incident should have been enough to cold-water the fiery Richard for the rest of the season, but fate seemed to have conspired against him—by the sixty-seventh game of the regular schedule, at Boston on March thirteen, Rocket's thirty-eight goals and thirty-six assists seemed to have the scoring championship he had so long desired firmly wrapped up. The fire of challenge was consuming the fellow, with six minutes to go in the game, when Canadiens' coach Irvin gambled as Boston drew a penalty. Yanking one's goaler for an extra forward with that much time to go is seldom done, but Canadiens were going for broke—they were racing to the wire, tied with Detroit for the league lead and intensely aware of the bonus one-thousand-dollars-per-man difference between ending second and first.

The mayhem started as ex-Canadien Hal Laycoe, then on the Bruin defence, high-sticked the Rocket, cutting the latter's head. Laycoe later charged that he had only reacted automatically when the Rocket hit him a blow on the glasses. Much of the melee was obscured by a cloud of confusion but it was clearly established that the Rocket did circle back, break his stick across Laycoe's back and sock linesman Cliff Thompson in the face. Referee Frank Udvari tossed a match penalty at Richard (Laycoe drew a major and a misconduct).

Campbell went into judicial conclave with all concerned, then shut off the world while he deliberated on further punishment; the match misconduct and automatic fines for the Laycoe part of the melee might have been enough but an assault on an official has to be given special consideration. Besides, there had been that other assault on an official in Toronto three months previously.

Montreal hockey fans and even non-fans were in a furore. The consensus of opinion seemed to be that a stiff fine, plus suspension for the remaining three games of the regular schedule, would be enough; this would likely cost Rocket his first scoring championship since team mates Geoffrion and Beliveau were right behind him. In addition, he personally could be hit hard financially if his suspension helped Canadiens to lose their slender one-game edge in the League title race and perhaps the Stanley Cup itself.

Campbell, however, decided "the time for probation or leniency is past." He suspended Richard from all games, both league and playoff, for the balance of the season. And all three most-feared things came to pass:

Rocket lost his biggest bid for the scoring crown by one point to Boom Boom Geoffrion, who was booed by his own Montreal fans when he scored the clincher.

Canadiens lost the league championship by the margin of a single game in an incredible final week. On March 13 Canadiens were one game ahead. On March 16, with Canadiens idle, Detroit tied the race. On March 17 the two teams met and the forfeited game went to Detroit. On March 19, with Detroit idle, Canadiens tied things up again. On March 20, in the final game of the schedule and with Canadiens at Detroit, Detroit goose-egged the dispirited Canadiens, 6-0.

Canadiens lost the Stanley Cup by a nose. While Detroit had been polishing off Toronto in four straight, semi-final games, Canadiens had eliminated Boston in five. The final series had gone to the seven-game limit with Detroit taking four.

There can be little doubt that, with everything being settled by the margin of a whisker, Rocket Richard's suspension was a crucial factor.

If ever there was a prize plot for building up hockey mob hysteria, the one leading up to the night of the good St. Patrick's feast day on March seventeenth, has to be it.

I'm still convinced that way back during the previous summer up high in the Sun Life Building in Montreal, a scheming Fate with a leer on her lips must have stood at the elbow of the designer of the forthcoming 1954/55 schedule. How else can one explain the booking of Detroit into Montreal Forum on that date when both the league and scoring titles would be up for grabs—only hours after the announcement of Rocket's suspension!

The designer of the schedule always insisted on doing the tricky job himself—President Clarence Sutherland Campbell was the man who drew it up. If that game had been scheduled for Detroit, it would likely have allowed time for simmering-down in Montreal, averted the city's wildest riot ever and saved him a sore jaw as well as a trip to the cleaners with an egg-strewn suit.

A Night to Remember

In the Canadiens' dressing-room, coach Dick Irvin thoughtfully inspected the charred canister that had housed the tear-gas bomb.

The bomb, massively smoky and tear-jerking, had jolted the Detroit-Canadiens game to a halt at the end of the first period and prompted the Montreal Fire Department to order evacuation of the Forum because of the panic menace.

"I have often seen Rocket Richard fill the Forum," mused Irvin, "but this is the first time I've seen him empty it."

Actually, the bomb was only one incident in the startling course of mob hysteria. In a way, the night to remember served a good purpose. I believe it gave the news media of Montreal—radio, television and press—a sobering realization of its awesome power in whipping up human emotions. A fellow named Hitler was a master at the art; but in Montreal nothing more was intended by the media than to go along with fan fever—to ride a good thing with public reaction to the Rocket's suspension. But it was startling to see how even fan fever can merge into mob hysteria.

It was also a gigantic example of how the Rocket could turn metropolitan Montreal upside down.

There had, of course, been the inexcusable prelude
of nasty and inflammatory accusations that led to
Richard's public apology and retirement (temporary)
from the sports-writing field. If the columns had been
under the by-line of some jerk named Joe, inflammatory
and sensation-hunting stuff would likely have had little
or no effect on the masses. But when it was by-lined by
their hockey idol it took on new significance—fans,
rallied out of loyalty to the campaign against alleged
injustice. When their idol apologized and said it had all
been unfounded, the "loyal" fans insisted he had been
"muzzled" and kept right on feeling done-wrong-by.

When Campbell announced the suspension, most
Montreal radio stations went overboard in giving "public
reaction" the big treatment in French and English. The
overwhelming majority of those rushing to yack were
pro-Richard. In listening to them it would seem that the
two officials, slugged by Richard within three months,
had really been the sinners.

The National Hockey League headquarters was del-
uged by crank calls. Several threatened anonymously to
"kill Campbell." One caller pledged to dynamite the
Gibraltar-like Sun Life edifice. Grocery chains were
amazed at the shoppers' venom directed at Campbell's
soups—although the link with the NHL prexy was a
matter of name only.

Fans jammed the Forum lobby to announce that they
would never again attend a hockey game there. Others
called to say they wouldn't even follow the NHL via
television. One woman warned the Forum that she would
be among a specially organized one thousand fans "who
will be there tonight to protest."

Loyal line mate Elmer Lach helped feed the flames
with: "They always tried to get the Rocket and now they
finally have."

Coach Irvin flatly tagged the suspension "an injustice."
In Ottawa, the Progressive-Conservative member for

Three Rivers, Leon Balcer, attempted to inject the suspension issue on a "question of privilege." The Liberal benches yelled for "Order!" and Speaker René Beaudoin ruled it out of order.

At the Forum that night of March seventeenth, the angry-mob feeling oozed from the walls as we entered. Campbell had said, in reply to questions, that he would be going to the game. Later when Mayor Jean Drapeau criticized him for going, Campbell blew his top. A former combat officer who had been assigned to serve on the prosecution staff at the Nuremberg war crime trials and an ex-NHL referee to boot, he snorted: "Does the mayor suggest I should have yielded to the intimidation of a few hoodlums?"

It was a nasty sight; throughout the first and only period of the game, Campbell and his fiancée Phyllis (now Mrs. Campbell) sat under a shower of eggs and assorted debris. When the period ended, a black-jacketed hoodlum rushed to Campbell's seat and hit him twice before running off. The other hoodlum had the tear-gas bomb, also meant for Campbell, but it went off prematurely in the promenade a short distance away.

The smoke billowed up to the Forum roof and people ran gasping for the exits. The lobby was soon filled with coughing, weeping fans. The public address system finally announced that the game had been forfeited; the crowd pouring from exits on all sides of the Forum seemed to flow around to the front of the building on St. Catherine Street. Now the hoodlums took over amid the dense crowd of people who were mainly standing around "just to see the fun."

The "fun" extended to shattering windows in front of the Forum as well as windows of stores located there. Then the mob marched eastward on St. Catherine Street, breaking more windows, upsetting cars, roughing-up bystanders and looting jewelry stores. The damage estimates soared above one hundred thousand dollars.

Thirty-seven men were arrested as well as some one
hundred juveniles—twenty-five of whom were held for
trial before the Social Welfare Court. It struck me as a
particularly revealing example of mob hysteria that a
student from a well-to-do Montreal family turned up next
day at a police station, emptied his pockets of watches
and jewelry snatched from behind a broken window and
confessed:

"I still don't know why I did it."

Across Canada the Richard Riot that should have
really become recorded in history as the Richard Fans
Riot took over the front pages. As far down as Florida
the usual stories on Canadian winter discomforts being
suffered in March were replaced by "the Canadien
Storm."

In far-off Germany, where the nation was still recover-
ing from the impact of the Penticton Vees—"Gashouse
Gang from the Okanagan"—in mangling their way
through the 1955 World Hockey Tournament climaxed
by the 5-0 steam-rollering of the reigning champion
Russian team, the Düsseldorf *Nachrichten* treated the
riot with a front-page sweepline. The report seemed to
be offered as evidence that what had just been seen in
Düsseldorf wasn't extraordinary at all—that turbulence
and Canadian hockey always went together. The Berliner
Morgenpost's two-column front-page story conveyed the
impression that war-scarred Berlin had been lucky to
escape complete demolition when the Vees played a pre-
tourney exhibition game there.

The Dublin papers, with tongue in cheek, commented
that French Canada had celebrated St. Patrick's Day with
much more vigour than had the Irish in Ireland. The
staid London press, long accustomed to blood-and-thun-
der soccer upheavals, were quite understanding about it
all but deplored the looting of stores. In Detroit, where
Canadiens would be closing out the schedule on Sunday
night, the papers were fretting over a report that fanatical

Canadien fans planned to make the trip and secrete another tear-gas bomb into the Olympia to force a retaliatory forfeited game (the home team is responsible for order).

In Montreal, the City Hall's august council was reduced to shambles. The resignation of Police Chief Tom Leggett was demanded but blanketed under pro-Leggett roars of protest. City Councillor Adeopat Crompt announced he would seek a warrant for the arrest of President Campbell on the grounds that he had "provoked" the riot. The City Attorney declared emphatically that the city wasn't liable for the damages. Campbell tagged rumours of his impending resignation as "utter rot." Merchants on St. Catherine Street loudly demanded more police protection for the Saturday night, March nineteenth, game; the Montreal Police promptly announced that a special force of detectives, more than two hundred and fifty strong, would be mingling with the crowds while the Fire Department would be standing by with hoses. Heated arguments raged in the abundant bistros of Montreal, with nobody on the fence; everybody was pro-Richard or pro-Campbell.

Calm came to the turbulent city only through the direct intervention of the Rocket himself.

He phoned Selke who later told me: "I might have been leery of going along with his suggestion that he make a personal appeal to the fans through radio and television, because of what he might say to make matters even worse; but Maurice was obviously subdued and awed by the effect of his actions. So I agreed to set it up if we would work out a statement together."

It was highly dramatic. The storied Canadiens' dressing room was transformed into a studio. Wan, weary and unsmiling, Richard sat behind a battery of microphones and under intensive floodlight glare. Behind him on the wall hung his No. 9 sweater. Speaking with obvious sincerity in French, then in English, he begged that no more harm be done, that everybody get behind "my team" to win against Rangers and Detroit.

"I will take my punishment," he told the vast, multi-million networks audience, "and come back next year to help the club and the younger players win the cup."

Which is exactly what he did with another spectacular scoring season: 71 points (38-33) in the regular seventy games followed by 14 (5-9) in the playoffs leading all the way to the Stanley Cup. He even reformed to some degree, cutting down his seasonal sin-bin time from 125 minutes to 113.

But it was done under a new coach, his old line mate, Toe Blake.

Dick Irvin had been a side-casualty of The Richard Riot. In many ways, Irvin and the Rocket were akin. Both raged with the fire to win and back in Irvin's own playing days, with Portland of the Pacific Coast League, Regina of the Western Canada Hockey League and finally with the Chicago Black Hawks (before becoming their coach in 1929), he had been not only a star scorer but a confirmed tangler with "bad men" of his era. So it was that the Rocket in turmoil found nothing but indignant sympathy from his coach.

When Selke decided it was time to probe deeply into the Rocket situation on direct orders of Senator Donat Raymond, then president of Canadiens, he went back to that December twenty-ninth row during the same season at Toronto. The movies of the game showed that the battle with Leafs' Bob Bailey, followed by the incident with linesman George Hayes, came only after Richard had skated to the Canadiens' bench where Irvin had said something to him. Richard had then turned away from the bench and skated into big trouble.

When the follow-up furore happened in Boston, Selke was in New York. It is no secret that Selke felt Irvin should have realized there was no excusing his player and that he should not have criticized all officialdom from

Campbell down. If ever Rocket needed advice to retire from the battle arena and lick wounds with an immediate apology, it was then.

After Canadiens, without Richard, were eliminated from the playoffs, Selke put it bluntly to Irvin: "You can't keep coaching Canadians after all this, Dick, but in recognition of the good years and services rendered, I am authorized to offer you a job in the organization, for life, at the same money you are now getting."

Thus ended Irvin's fifteen-season stint as Canadiens' pilot, during which he took them to four league championships and three Stanley Cup wins. Typically, he turned down the cushy job-for-life offer from Canadiens for the challenge of the coaching job with the then last-place Chicago Black Hawks. There was a very special appeal there for him: it was the club he had played for and once coached. Perhaps there was about it all a sense of rejuvenation at the age of sixty-three.

Dick spent one season at the Hawks' helm. He didn't get them out of the cellar; and illness was eating at him. He died in Montreal in May, 1957. One year later he was named to the Hockey Hall of Fame—as a player. Dick would have liked that because even while the rest of him was behind the bench, his heart was always out on the ice.

He was wonderful copy for us press guys. He once told me that on looking back over fourteen hundred National Hockey League games, and some two hundred different players handled during that time, there was only one night he felt afraid to use a player.

That night was March 22, 1952. The place was Detroit's Olympia. The player was Rocket Richard.

Oddly enough, it was a "nothing" game—last game of the schedule, the outcome of which could not alter the standings for the playoffs. But the spotlight was on Detroit's great Gordie Howe who had scored forty-nine goals to date and needed only one more to tie the then seasonal record of fifty goals set by the Rocket in 1944/45. Before leaving Montreal, Irvin had told us he was thinking of shifting Richard from right wing over to left wing for the game so he'd have the honour of hand-cuffing Howe in person.

"It seemed a good idea at the time," Irvin grinned in retrospect, "but when I looked at the Rocket in the dressing room before the game my heart sank. He was dour and withdrawn from the usual chatter and ribbing. Nine years of seeing Richard storms brewing warned me to take some preventative action but what? If I left him on Howe, there could be an explosion; if I left him over on his own wing and Howe tied, maybe even broke, Richard's beloved record, what would it do to his morale, the team morale? I decided to gamble and let things ride."

Within minutes Richard caught Howe with a body-check that draped the Red Wing superstar across the boards and the Detroit crowd roared in wrath. Irvin decided to act; he told Rocket to lay off Howe because he would be a target for watchful refereeing eyes and ordered Bert Olmstead and Johnny McCormack of another line to concentrate on stopping Howe "regardless of the outcome of the game." Irvin even told Olmstead to escort Howe to the Detroit bench on player changes in the hope of getting Howe riled.

"Yet, despite my precautions," Irvin continued, "every time I looked up it seemed Rocket was hellbenting for Howe again—so quickly do the lines tumble over the boards in modern hockey that I'd lose track. Somehow the game ended without chaos. It was a tie but I hardly thought of it—the big thing was that Howe hadn't scored, in fact he had been held to only one at all dangerous shot. In the dressing room you'd think we had already won the Stanley Cup—the Rocket was romping around like a kid and goaler Gerry McNeil was yelling. 'Hi Rock—Howe has to start at No. 1 again!' "

Rocket repaid Irvin and his team mates about three weeks later on April 8, 1952, with what is still recognized as the greatest goal ever scored in Stanley Cup competition.

It was the seventh and last game of the bruising semifinals against Boston Bruins. In the second period Rocket, going in at express speed, was knocked off balance by Leo LaBine and plunged head-first into defenceman Bill Quackenbush's knee. From the Forum press box high up near the roof it looked like Rocket's neck was broken; his head had twisted almost completely around and he lay absolutely still on the ice, completely out. He was carried off. Six stitches were needed to close up a deep cut on his forehead and he was still somewhat befuddled in the third period when he insisted on returning to the bench. The score was 1-1 and there were four minutes of regular time left.

"I'm all right," he told Irvin.

Elmer Lach told me: "I caught Rocket squinting up at the clock and asked him what was the matter. He told me his eyes weren't in focus but just then it was time for a line change and over we went."

You read about such goals in fiction, but the 2-1 winner was actually scored by the Rocket on an end-to-end rush in which he went through or around all six Boston Bruins on the ice. In the course of that long rush there had to be opportunities to pass, but we didn't know the reason he held on to the puck all the breathtaking way was that his fuzzy eyes couldn't pick up a receiver.

From the bench, Rocket skated down beside his own net where he took a pass from defenceman Butch Bouchard, eluded a forechecking Bruin winger and veered toward centre ice. He managed to sweep left of the centre's reaching pokecheck then spurted away from the other Bruin winger and across the Boston blueline.

Playing instinctively, he aimed for his favourite "button-hook" play, whirling to the right and attempting to circle

Quackenbush with the help of a left-arm shove. But the
veteran Quackenbush rode him off, almost to the boards.

However, it was still high-speed action and again
Richard surged into Quackenbush. This time he got by;
but Bob Armstrong, the other Bruin defenceman, charged
forward to stop Richard. Richard shoved the puck out
to his right, literally brushed Armstrong aside and
whirled in front of the net. Goaler Sugar Jim Henry,
squinting through two black eyes and from behind a
broken nose suffered earlier in the game, dove fran-
tically. Richard pulled the puck aside and blasted into
the net.

For the first time I really appreciated the eerie description of Richard written by Nobel Prize novelist William
Faulkner in *Sports Illustrated.* Faulkner's debut as a
hockey observer at Madison Square Garden saw a 7-1
Canadien victory and through it all "one single figure,
a man called Richard" struck him most forcefully with a
"passionate, glittering, fatal alien quality of snakes."

Has there ever been, before or since, a player in the
hockey Big Time who could "call his shots" as did Rocket
Richard?

There have been, and still are, stars and superstars
who come up with big goals but it is another thing altogether to deliver a required number of goals on a
required date as predicted.

Two such rousing nights in 1952 and 1958 still send
fireworks through my hockey memories:

It really wasn't fair—the way the Toronto papers laid
the pressure on Rocket Richard for the game there on
October 29, 1952.

The *Telegram, Globe and Mail* and *Daily Star* all highlighted that day the assault on Nelson Stewart's eleven-
year-old record of 324 goals to be made that night by
Rocket Richard whose career total in regular-season play
stood at 322.

It was significant that no paper considered whether he'd get one goal—it was, would he get two to tie the record? The challenge was enormous and 14,069 vociferously biased, anti-Richard fans got into the spirit of things by booing every time he got near the puck. They cheered when he was dumped by defenceman Tim Horton. They howled indignantly at referee Red Storey for missing a face-poking action by Richard at Max Bentley.

At 11:01 of the first period Richard took a blueline pass from Elmer Lach, deked the defence and blistered a shot by Leaf goalie Harry Lumley. Goal No. 323.

Six minutes later, there was a wild melee in front of the Toronto net as the Rocket piled up both defencemen, a forward and Lumley. On went the red light for Goal No. 324.

The Rocket had delivered the two goals as per challenge order within seventeen minutes and seven seconds!

Nor was it fair that Montreal fans, 14,528 of them, should have jammed the Forum on the night of February 20, 1958, in open expectation of a multi-goal Rocket explosion.

After all the man was appearing after a three-month layoff; on November thirteenth at Toronto he had suffered a partially severed Achilles tendon that was said, at the time, to mark the end of a fabulous career. Prior to the layoff, he had played only fourteen games. But he fooled the medicos and the experts and was back, at the age of thirty-six, with the greeting of thousands resounding in his ears.

Canadiens blanked the Bruins that night, 4-0. Two of the four goals were Rocket thrillers—both on an assist from brother Henri Richard. The second goal saw the Rocket, his cover and the Bruin goaler all end up in the net with the puck.

As if to apologize for lost time, or maybe just to prove he wasn't at all ready for the armchair and slippers being suggested for him a few months previously, Rocket personally bombed the Detroit Red Wings out of the semi-finals in four-straight with a total of seven goals. In the final series against Boston Bruins, he counted four more goals as Canadiens took the Cup.

There was only one indication around this time that age was creeping up on the Rocket; he wasn't busting up whole teams physically any more.

Like that night in early 1953 when he went into a game against Detroit Red Wings with an obvious "mad" on. He drew a minor penalty for crosschecking tough Ted Lindsay dizzy. He came out of the penalty box and high-sticked Glenn Skov for another minor. In a short time he was serving a third minor for charging Red Kelly. When Rocket returned to action the Detroit "policeman," Marcel Pronovost, decided it was time to apply his six-foot, one hunded and ninety pound physique at putting Rocket in his place. Pronovost ended with a broken jaw and six missing teeth. Richard drew a major penalty on that one, then a misconduct when he hopped from the sin-bin to take another poke at Lindsay.

In the twenty-minute period, Rocket picked up a total of twenty-one minutes in penalties.

I'm certainly not trying to hail that performance as laudable but the man sure showed us many ways to wreck NHL teams.

But the end was nearing. The heart was still there but the legs weren't what they used to be—defencemen were now getting to the Rocket with bodychecks that made us wince.

The influence of Hector (Toe) Blake was tremendous. Aside from turning out to be a better coach than any of us imagined he would, he had the deep-down respect of his old line mate.

Blake had a thirteen-season record of 260 goals and 339 assists in 629 regular and playoff games with the old

Montreal Maroons and the Canadiens. He was a winner of the Hart (most valuable player) Trophy in 1938/39 and, astonishingly for a player with an early chip-on-shoulder reputation, the Lady Byng (gentlemanly conduct plus effective play) Trophy in 1945/46.

His pre-NHL grooming as coach came with Houston in the old United States Hockey League, Buffalo in the American League and Valleyfield in the Quebec League. He was elected to the Hockey Hall of Fame in June, 1966.

From this immense background, Blake guided Canadiens to eight first-place finishes and seven Stanley Cups. The same background produced a calming effect on the fiery Rocket when Blake would say:

"You don't have to prove anything to us in the dressing-room or to the fans out there, Rock; don't let them (the opponents) suck you into penalties."

There was, at the time, another happy influence on the Rocket in his former hardrock team mate of the defence brigade, Kenny Reardon. Kenny had been raised to the vice-presidency by Selke but he wasn't averse to busting in on dressing-room moments of tension. Such as one night at Madison Square Garden when Lou Fontinato, then the Rangers' "bad man," had cut open Rocket's eye with a punch during a wild melee at the end of a period.

Richard was sitting and seething in the room when Kenny rushed in to sit beside him: "It was a lucky punch, Rock, and we don't want you to do anything about it. We can't risk losing you—for the team's sake, forget it."

The Rocket simply glowered back but the message had been received—the team angle always got to him.

The end came at the end of the 1959/60 season. He was still a better-than-good player with a 19-16 record from the fifty-one games he played during the regular schedule and 1-3 in eight playoff games. But anything less than stardom wasn't enough for Rocket Richard.

When he picked up the puck after his final goal—the playoffer score with assists by Henri Richard and Dickie Moore—on April 12, 1960, at Maple Leaf Gardens, we wondered if it was significant.

In the dressing-room, he shrugged it all off with: "I always regretted that I didn't keep the puck from my first playoff goal but, at least, I have the one with which I scored my eighty-second. If I don't retire, and score another playoff goal, I'll give this one to some kid."

He worked hard at conditioning during the summer, passed his thirty-ninth birthday on August fourth, and reported bronzed and fit-looking to training camp. But Selke saw something during that camp; he had long pledged that he wouldn't allow Rocket to suffer the humiliations of a burned-out veteran. He called the Rocket to his office.

It wasn't until seven years later, in 1967, that Rocket Richard admitted to me: "I didn't really feel I was ready to retire—I'm still sure I could have lasted another season or two. The deciding factor came when Selke offered me the same salary to keep on as Goodwill Ambassador for Canadiens while—to use Selke's words—my 'image' was still high. In my heart I was a little sick about quitting but I knew he was right and the constant threat of injuries was beginning to bother me."

Beginning to bother him? This man had missed a total of 169 games through injuries in hockey. A total of three leg fractures. A right elbow injury that demanded surgery to remove chips. A left wrist fracture. A near-severing of an Achilles tendon. A depressed fracture of the facial bone. A groin injury that continued to bother him. Hundreds of stitches. Teeth knocked out. Painful sprains and bruises beyond count. Sleepless nights on trains, nursing ice-packs.

Yet his retirement stunned us all when it was announced in mid-September at a massive press conference held at the Queen Elizabeth Hotel. It was deeply emotional; the hard-boiled press, radio and television guys stood around with lump in throat as he spoke in a voice filled with grief:

"I can never repay hockey for what it has done for me and my family."

His new job started off with an odd but immensely flattering twist. Czechoslovakia invited him and his wife to attend the Spartakiade events of the 1960 summer sports festival in Prague and they were astounded to find he was an idol over there—although Czechoslovakia had never seen him play. As far back as 1956, a Moscow magazine with two million circulation had given a feature spread to the brothers Richard—Maurice and Henri.

But years bring changes to men and their thinking.

The goodwill-ambassadorship job—with its endless routine of personal appearances at dinners and sports events, plane trips, thousands of speeches he always felt awkward about making, the strain of giving diplomatic answers to ticklish questions involving Canadiens—began losing glamour.

In 1966 he was made Assistant to the President, now J. David Molson. Things didn't pan out. From the management viewpoint the job entailed undertaking a program in which Rocket would cover all facets of the organization. It would also require a lot of office time. From Rocket's viewpoint it "wasn't much of a job"; office routine was not for him especially when his dynamic spirit longed for the vast Quebec northland and its fishing and hunting, or the superbly relaxing influence of a sunny summer afternoon on the golf course. Besides, he had a prospering oil business and other sidelines going for him after he sold out his tavern.

Rocket handed in his resignation, thus giving up a five-figure annual stipend but continuing on friendly terms with management. President Molson told me: "Rocket will continue to handle special goodwill jobs for us on a fee basis."

In July, 1967, as part of Canada's Centennial Year, the first ranks of a new Order of Canada were formed to recognize outstanding achievement. Among the greats of the land so signally honoured was one hockey star, Rocket Richard. Appropriately enough, the Medal of Service he may proudly wear like a military decoration, pinned on the left side of his chest, has a ribbon with stripes of red and white. Henceforth, behind his name he may use the initials, SM.

He still remains a fervent Canadien fan, attending all games when he is in town. He appears frequently on television in between-periods interviews. His name continues to appear atop ghost-written columns in the French press. But, most satisfactory of all for his still fervent fans, is that Rocket Richard is still playing hockey. At age fifty, he is paying to play with the Quebec NHL Old Timers; he and Lach and Reardon, Butch Bouchard, Glen Harmon, Ken Mosdell, and many others, chip in for ice time from ten to eleven thirty on Monday nights for practices at the old Lachine Arena. They buy their own equipment, chip in for the beer and sandwiches afterwards. Their games on an expenses-only basis raise thousands of dollars for charity annually.

Even there, playing watered-down hockey that bans the slapshot and bodychecking (to avert injuries), he shows flashes of the old Rocket.

One Sunday in 1966/67 goalie Jacques Plante (then retired before his 1968 comeback with St. Louis Blues) failed to appear with the team for a benefit at Sudbury. Plante had been among the old stars most heavily publicized and his absence, for personal reasons, forced the team to accept a local goalie who failed to stop a shot in the warm-up period. The Rocket took the microphone and apologized in a rather irritated way for Plante's absence, finishing with, "We will do the best we can."

The goalie did well and Rocket scored four goals. His

team won and the packed house was standing most of the time.

Typically, too, he still wars against whole cities. As I write, he and Quebec City, capital of his native province, aren't speaking. It all goes back a way.

Canadiens went in there for an exhibition game against a Canadian Navy team around the end of World War II. A local referee began getting on Rocket's rather brittle nerves. Rocket told him to quit "ruining" the game with piddling penalties. On the next play the Rocket drew one of those piddling penalties and his team had to shove him into the penalty box where Rocket stood gesturing for the referee to come closer. The ref, with a potential misconduct penalty written all over his face, came within a few feet to ask: "What do you want?"

The Rocket poked the blade of his stick under the cord holding the ref's whistle around his neck, pulled the ref toward him with his left hand and socked him with his right. The ref landed on his rear and slid halfway to mid-ice.

Rocket Richard retired from the scene under a barrage of boos.

The next incident involved his sports column where he went to the defence of brother Henri, then a junior, and called the Quebec City fans "bandits."

Finally came the crusher incident as described to me by ex-referee Red Storey. He was doing a volunteer stint of officiating at a peewee tournament in Quebec City where Maurice Richard, junior, was competing with a team from Montreal. Says Storey:

When the public address system introduced "No. 9, Rocket Richard, junior," the crowd of some fifteen thousand booed. I saw tears in the kid's eyes and tried to comfort him but he could talk no English and I could talk no French. Anyway, I don't think he liked referees any better than his Dad did.

That did it for keeps with Rocket, senior. When, in

1967, his Old Timers team was invited to play there, he flatly refused to go:

"Charity or no charity, I won't do anything to make those Quebec City fans happy."

On the morning of March 31, 1967, Montrealers paused over their breakfasts to stare at a headline in the *Gazette*:

ROCKET GETS TWO GOALS IN 6-2 WIN

The dateline of the Reuters' report was Chamonix, France, historic site of the first Olympic Winter Games in 1924. Somehow, a team from the old Montreal Depression Hockey League—a loop formed many years ago with retired pros and senior amateurs interested purely in keeping in shape—had gone abroad on a tour without any publicity fanfare. The first that Montreal knew about it was in this 6-2 win over "the French champion Chamonix hockey club."

Later we learned that the Rocket was amazed—and delighted—to be hailed as an ageless great in the France that had never seen him play. In Grenoble, his face appeared on posters, and residents being geared for the 1968 Winter Olympics so jammed the rink that a second game had to be played the next night to handle the overflow. He responded to the tribute in typical fashion: during eight games played in eleven days in France he scored eighteen goals. But tourist Rocket Richard also placed his "rhubarb trademark" on the triumphant visit. For violating the rule forbidding amateurs to play against professionals, present or past, the French Ice Hockey Federation suspended all teams he played against—as well as the referees—for two years.

The scales and his barber testify to a changing Rocket, but Montreal knows there has been only one real change in the "for fun" sunset stage of his hockey career; whereas Rocket rhubarbs used to be restricted to North America, they have now taken on an inter-continental dimension.

Mr. Everything

There's a story that's still told for the benefit of cub reporters around newspaper offices, although it dates back to 1889 and the grim Johnstown, Pa., flood disaster (twenty-two hundred lives lost).

The first tip-off of mounting tragedy in the valley reached the nearest major newspaper office in the small morning hours. The night editor found only one sleepy reporter, a raw cub, in the editorial room. The cub was told to get to the tragedy and accumulate all available material before being relieved by senior reporters. He got to the valley but was promptly shut off from the rest of the world by the rampaging waters.

The first edition deadline passed with the distraught editor having only vague but disquieting information to work on. Finally a weak telegraph link with the valley was made and the cub's report began trickling through:

"God sits upon a lonely mountaintop tonight and gazes down upon a desolate Johnstown. The roar of swirling waters echoes in the. . . ."

Emitting some blue comment, the editor glanced disgustedly through the scented saga then thumped out a telegram to the cub: "Okay. Forget flood. Interview God. Rush pictures."

The story insists on coming to mind when I find myself involved with a hockey game when hockey's "Mr. Everything," Jean Beliveau, is around. So exalted is the "image" projected by him that a writer is often tempted to regard the game and the score as secondary.

He is the only superstar—repeat, the only one—I have known who has skated throughout starring, headline-haunted junior, senior and National Hockey League years literally above criticism. Not once have I heard even an opposing executive, fan or player, say anything about him other than laudatory. Even when he breaks their hearts they unite in praise. Off the ice, his handsome features atop an erect, six-foot-three, 205-pound frame encased in flawlessly tailored clothes, reflect quiet dignity. His bilingual remarks before frequent microphones are invariably in good taste and a credit to professional hockey.

Rocket Richard, of course, stormed his way through a controversial career in which bitter booing and delirious cheering mingled for background music. Even Detroit's Gordie Howe draws a share of caustic comment from opposing players: "Why don't the referees watch that big so-and-so's elbows?" And from opposing coaches: "That Howe brainwashes referees at the start of every game by asking how's the wife and kids, did the ref recover from the flu he had last week in Chicago and such hogwash to create the good-guy image." Certainly the sarcastic gentlemen of the opposition had something to I-told-you-so about after Howe did that monumental face-lifting job on the then Ranger badman, Lou Fontinato, in New York. *Life* magazine came out with an admiring saga that somehow conveyed the impression that poor Lou was an arch-villain who should have been grateful for escaping with his life.

But Jean Beliveau has always been a hero with everybody, the fan's idol, the hockey player's player. The fact that he has spent the equivalent of more than twenty full games in the penalty boxes of the NHL never seems to creep into articles about him—other stars get rapped for such sin-bin sojourning, but whatever spots of nastiness Jean gets involved in seem to be dismissed as excusable retaliation for unfair and illegal tactics employed by uncouth covers.

When his errant slapshot, during an All-Star game some years ago kayoed my wife, Frances, and left an eight-stitch gash beside her left eye, she pardoned him promptly, raved over his two dozen roses and joyfully served him a VIP lunch when he dropped into the house to sympathize.

Even when he hits a serious scoring slump, "Mr. Everything" emerges into joy unconfined—as for example on the night of December 3, 1966, at the Montreal Forum.

Unbelievable as it was to his ardent aficionados, this superdenter of goal twine who had scored 387 regular-season goals and 55 playoff screamers had gone throughout the preseason exhibition games and into this fourteenth scheduled game without scoring a single goal.

During the intermission between the first and second periods, Beliveau appeared on television with Canada's Prime Minister Lester Pearson. Courteously, the Prime Minister inquired about the slump and finished with: "I feel you will break it tonight, Jean." Smilingly, he promised he would try especially hard for the honoured guest.

True to his word, the Canadiens' captain surged into action against the then league-leading Chicago Black Hawks and bulled his way through the defence and into point-blank range on goaler Dennis DeJordy, who stopped the shot. Jean got the rebound and fired again. Again DeJordy stopped him. Again Jean got the puck and this time there was no stopping him—as the near-frantic DeJordy sprawled to save, Jean drove the rubber over him and into the net.

It took four minutes to clear the ice as the fans showered everything throwable in tribute—like aficionados do with their favoured matador in the bull ring at Madrid. Fellow Canadiens circled to slap his shoulders and hug him—you'd think he had scored another Stanley Cup winner instead of the "insurance goal" in a 3-1 Canadien win.

To the gathered press in the jammed dressing room after the game, Jean said: "That goal was my biggest thrill—imagine the fans sticking with me like they did!"

As for the exultant Prime Minister Pearson, himself a better-than-good hockey player of bygone years, he modestly refused to accept all the credit for the surge from the doldrums: "Afer all, I didn't actually score the goal. . . ."

But coach Toe Blake was under no illusions. "I wonder," he said, "if Ottawa needs Mr. Pearson as much as I do around here?"

It was somewhat reminiscent of the first time I interviewed Jean Beliveau in Quebec City in October, 1952. My editors at *Weekend Magazine* had decided on the full treatment—colour cover and all—under the heading: "He's Hockey's Most-Wanted." Jean was still with the Quebec Aces, a senior and officially amateur club that had allegedly donated some forty thousand dollars toward the lad's living expenses. The magnificent Auditorium at Quebec City was known as "Chateau Beliveau."

We drove from the auditorium in a swank, cream-coloured convertible, the second car presented to the twenty-one-year-old whiz by his admiring fans (the first had been presented at age nineteen). It bore a special Quebec license plate with the number "2 B"; the then Quebec premier, Maurice Duplessis had "1 B."

Jean parked his convertible directly in front of the main entrance of the famed Chateau Frontenac Hotel and we went up to my room. He poured himself a beer and was in the act of lighting up a cigar when there came a knock on the door. I opened it and in walked a Quebec City policeman. Taking off his fur cap, the cop said in French:

"If you let me have your key, Jean, I'll park your car."

Without interrupting his discussion, Jean threw the cop his keys. The cop backed out of the room apologetically. Frankly, I was awed—but I shouldn't have been.

There was a story then going the rounds in the ancient capital that insisted a local school teacher had asked his teenager class to name the great leader who captured Quebec City and when. Only a few named Britain's General Wolfe, in 1759. All the rest wrote: "Jean Beliveau in 1951/52".

In 1947/48 he made his debut in Junior-B calibre hockey at Victoriaville, Que., and scored forty-seven goals as well as assisting on twenty-one others in half a season. The next season, in Junior-A company, he scored forty-eight, had twenty-seven assists. In 1949/50 with the Quebec Junior Citadels he had thirty-five goals and forty-five assists. In 1950/51, still with the Citadels, he tore the league apart with sixty-one goals and sixty-three assists, followed by twenty-two playoff goals.

During that season the club's working-agreement big brother of the National Hockey League, Les Canadiens, brought up the nineteen-year-old sensation for a two-game test. He scored one goal, assisted on another. It was agreed that the teenager was good but just how good? Canadiens wanted to see him in action in senior company before making a firm offer.

Canadiens got their chance to look the next season—and were left breathless.

Beliveau whirled into senior company with a whoosh. In that first season with Quebec Aces, 1951/52, Jean topped the Quebec Senior Hockey League with forty-eight goals and thirty-eight assists.

In twenty playoff games he scored twenty-one goals as Aces bulldozed through to the Alexander Cup (Canadian senior title). He was voted to the first All-Star team, he was named rookie of the year, he was tagged "best pro prospect."

Canadiens decided to give that tag a full-dress test during the next season, 1952/53, and invited him "up" for three games.

In the three games Jean scored five goals!

One of the games saw him score the "hat trick"— three goals—against the New York Rangers. By way of illustrating his versatility, Jean employed three different techniques; one goal came off a long slapshot, another followed a feint, the third climaxed the circling of a Ranger defenceman as if there was nobody there.

Canadiens went on to win the Stanley Cup that season without Beliveau but the Montreal Forum natives were restless. General Manager Frank Selke later put it in a nutshell: "Even with the Stanley Cup in our cupboard, how could we long continue to convince Montreal fans that we had the best hockey players in the world while Beliveau was in Quebec?"

Meanwhile, Quebec was getting increasingly jittery. By now it was obvious that they had a tiger by the tail. The entire Quebec Senior Hockey League's prosperity hinged on one player; the Beliveau name was drawing crowds of fifteen thousand at home and capacity crowds on the road. When he missed a game through injury or illness, the rinks were half full. One menace had been already averted the expensive way—as Beliveau approached the junior age limit of exposure to some legal-but-tricky pro grab, the QSHL made him "untouchable" by labelling the entire league "professional."

But the explosive, three-game NHL test had shown even the most optimistic Quebecker that they couldn't hold on to their tiger's tail much longer. Coach "Punch" Imlach of the Aces (now general manager and coach of Toronto Maple Leafs) dropped a remark at this stage that left the fans of the six NHL cities aghast:

"The NHL certainly must know by now that my boy rates only with Gordie Howe and Rocket Richard in their league."

There was some derisive snorting by the NHL executives but it was apparent, very apparent, that Imlach's "boy" was better than good. Tall and 235 pounds in full hockey gear, possessor of a "heavy" slapshot that was usually dead on the net, he propelled it with a short, quick backswing to allow would-be blockers little chance to get set. His long skating stride carried a deceptive change of pace. He could shift opposing defencemen out of position. Under full steam one felt he was virtually impossible to stop when a Big Try was called for.

In Montreal, the Canadiens' brass drew up a contract that was then unprecedented.

Beliveau's intimates said it was for fifty-three thousand dollars for three years, breaking down as follows: twenty thousand dollars to sign, ten thousand dollars for the first season, eleven thousand dollars for the second and twelve thousand dollars for the third. In addition, of course, there were special bonus clauses, provisions for playoff splits, et cetera.

Ever so politely, Beliveau rejected the contract.

The Canadiens and Montreal fans were left in a state of shock. Everybody was asking: "Just WHAT does he want?"

That's when I interviewed him in the Chateau Frontenac and asked if he wanted to achieve every hockey player's dream and play in the NHL?

"Of course I do," he replied, "but—".

The emphasized "but" presented a roadblock I couldn't pass. I tried to circle it by asking if he had ever seen the storied Madison Square Garden? He shook his head. Well, didn't he want to see it?

"Sure," he said, "in the summer time."

But what had to happen did, the next season. Senator Donat Raymond, now deceased, was then president of

Canadiens and as rabid a fan as anybody in town. There came a day when he could stand it no longer and ordered General Manager Frank Selke to sign Beliveau in October, 1953.

When it all came to pass in an uproar of camera flash bulbs, panting press and bubbling broadcasters, the beaming Frank Selke was asked how he had achieved the miracle?

"It was really simple," he replied modestly, "all I did was open the Forum vault and say, 'Help yourself, Jean'."

Actually, Jean didn't quite clean out the vault—he took only one hundred and ten thousand dollars to go with what he had demanded, a five-year contract plus bonus clauses.

Selke's office was as crowded as New Year's Eve on Times Square, and just as noisy. Amid the unprecedented traffic jam caused by press, radio and television people and the cameramen, was a special Beliveau adviser from a trust company. Selke had countered with an expert from the income tax office. Beliveau had tried to follow the advice of his father (a foreman with the Shawinigan Water and Power at Victoriaville, Que.) who told Jean to refuse a contract with small print: "Three lines are always enough—and no lawyers."

But Jean was no mere hockey player signing a routine contract.

For years as an amateur he had been drawing the equivalent of a bank president's salary as expense money. The magic of his name had meant almost half a million cash customers annually at "Chateau Beliveau." He had linked up with several profitable enterprises such as the Laval Dairy which promoted him on trucks and via a weekly radio show from various church halls. Even politicians in the city, capital of Quebec Province, learned not to try bucking Beliveau popularity.

One sunny Sunday afternoon in the summer of 1952, Premier Maurice Duplessis and a wide range of dignitaries formally opened a new road over storied Quebec Bridge. Although the publicity tub-thumpers had worked overtime, a disappointing crowd turned out. Somebody had goofed by underestimating a rival attraction.

At the same time, across the city, a curb service ice cream spot, *La Dame Blanche* (the White Lady) was also being formally opened and Jean Beliveau was on hand to give out free ice cream cones. A crowd of seven thousand swamped the area.

What finally prompted Jean to leave the beloved Quebec City that he just about owned? What could make him trade his established superstar status with the QSHL for the vastly sterner NHL and possible mediocrity with the reigning hockey champions of the world?

Money wasn't the key reason because his pay cheques from the Aces and other interests already represented a formidable figure. More pay would add up to little more in a higher income tax bracket.

I believed then, and still do, that the big influence was a close friend, Emile Couture.

Hockey-wise, Emile was just another personable fellow mingling in amateur hockey circles. He had been good enough for a tryout with the Aces but an eye injury cut short his potential playing career. A respected young businessman as well, he had arranged the Laval Dairy contact for Jean and acted as middleman between the Aces and Jean getting the latter to move up early to the senior team.

However, friendship alone didn't make Emile so special—it was the revelation of just why Emile had received the British Empire Medal after the war without any accompanying explanation. Those who knew Emile had been flabbergasted because, although passed A-1 medically, he had never left a soft army job in Canada. When asked about the high decoration he would simply give with a smiling shrug: "Who can ever figure out why those things are given out?"

The incredible story just had to break eventually.

The truth was that Staff Sergeant E. Couture, No. E5930, of the famed Royal 22nd Regiment of Quebec, had actually learned the complete D-Day Invasion Plan ten months before June 6, 1944. The B.E.M. award had been given him for keeping the staggering secret shared only with Prime Minister Churchill, President Roosevelt and the absolute upper echelons of the Allied High Command.

His knowledge of not only the "when" of invasion but also the "where," the "how" and even the "by whom" left the worried High Command with one of two choices.

One was to shelve the whole plan and draft an entirely new one at a cost of possibly many months' delay and millions of dollars. The other was to go ahead, trusting that Couture would keep mum. They couldn't lock him up for the duration; aside from the injustice, such an action would undoubtedly attract unusual interest and even prompt the enemy to get a spy to him inside jail.

It was decided to trust Sergeant Couture for two reasons. Firstly, he had been cleared as a top security risk, a single man of moderate living habits. Secondly, there was the statement he made to the Emergency High Command Committee.

"None of your security precautions," he told them, "could insure my silence as completely as the knowledge that my talking might imperil the lives of my two brothers, both of whom are now captains overseas in training for the invasion."

Sergeant Couture had been one of only two army men allowed on the Secret Floor (third floor of the Chateau Frontenac) together with Royal Canadian Mounted Police personnel during the invasion-planning Quebec Conference of August, 1943. He was in charge of purchasing all office equipment and stationery for the conference and had been ordered to remove several desks whose occupants had been moved. It was while at this, that he came across a loose-leaf book left in a drawer. He put it in a clothes cupboard for the time being and went on shifting the desks.

Later, while preparing to leave for the night, he looked casually at the loose-leaf book, concluded it was merely a "sort of agenda," and thought it must have been discarded. He adds:

"I knew it was against the rules but I was tempted to see how a conference of such historic significance was conducted. I carried it out with me that night—in fairness to the RCMP guards it must be remembered that they were accustomed to seeing me carrying things."

He drove out to the Lake Beauport quarters he shared with three other army men, had supper, donned pyjamas and settled in bed with the book. To his intense horror, Emile realized he was reading Top Secret data—the invasion date ("between June 2 and June 8, 1944, with a listing of weather prospects"), the command appointments to be made (including General Montgomery and Admiral Louis Mountbatten) as well as the points of attack and by what forces and how many men of what armies. Finally, there was a "Plan X" which, it was estimated, would finish off Japan in 1945. Couture was intrigued by a notation to the effect that "if Plan X does not work, Japan will be starved by blockade." (Long after, he recalled there was no mention of the atom bomb —apparently not perfected as yet.)

Emile tucked the loose-leaf book under him in the bed and turned out the light. He slept fitfully, realizing that his knowledge could cause him to be interned for the war in a form of solitary confinement as protection of the secret. The next morning, he skipped breakfast and dashed out before his three army mates were up—with the invasion plans tucked in the spare tire of his car.

Even at the early hour he found Chateau Frontenac in a state of turmoil. Whatever member of the high brass (or was it Roosevelt or Churchill?) had committed the gross error, it had been reported and the hotel was alive with emergency meetings. Were the plans already in enemy hands? Should the conference be started over?

Emile had a problem. He could surrender the plans only to "the highest brass I could reach." He thought of Admiral of the Fleet Sir Dudley Pound, who had often spoken to him pleasantly; but Sir Dudley's secretary simply waved him away—the admiral was impossibly busy. So were six other bigwigs Emile tried to reach. Finally, in mounting desperation, Emile parked himself outside the office of Brigadier Edmond Blais, commanding officer of Military District No. 5. The irritated brigadier, figuring Emile was after a promotion, brusquely ordered him to go away. After two hours, Emile finally barged in on the brigadier, shut the door and begged:

"Please glance at this, Sir!"

One glance was enough. Emile found himself quizzed for hours by "more brass than I knew existed."

When it was decided to make what was really a king-sized gamble and leave Emile loose and at his job, there were constant security checks.

"One was a nifty," laughed Emile when we talked about it after the war. "Knowing I always read the sport pages, an ad was planted one day offering five thousand dollars in war bonds for the guess closest to the invasion date. All you had to do was send in your guess with a five-dollar bill to a certain box number in Ottawa. I couldn't resist the temptation to throw a scare into the brigadier (who later was also decorated for helping to keep the secret) and showed him the ad, asking if he'd like to join me in making some money. He exploded before realizing I was kidding."

There was only one time when Emile almost spilled the beans. On stepping hurriedly into an elevator in the Chateau Frontenac he found himself face to face with Lord Louis Mountbatten. They were on speaking terms and he gave Emile a sunny greeting.

"I was just about to reply with warm congratulations on his appointment as Supreme Allied Commander in Southeast Asia when a sudden thought caused me to shut off the words," says Emile. "It dawned on me that he might not know of his appointment for a week or so."

It was small wonder that young Jean Beliveau found Emile Couture not only an interesting person but one whose dependability had been recognized internationally. Emile's handling of the signing that brought Beliveau to the Aces in a way that left everybody happy prompted the Aces' management to make him president of the Quebec Junior Frontenacs.

Emile had also become friendly with Canadiens' Frank Selke through a personal happening. Paul Bibeault, formerly a goalkeeper with Aces and then with Toronto Maple Leafs, had become engaged to Selke's daughter and invited Emile to act as best man. Selke got to like him; when Canadiens decided to go all-out for Beliveau, it was Emile whose cooperation Selke sought.

"It would be wrong for me to take more than a share of the credit for major hockey's most important signing," Emile later stressed to me, "because Jean had matured beyond his years and weighed the conflicting opinions of many advisers very carefully. But I did know, and stressed to Mr. Selke, that Jean sought above all security in a profession notoriously insecure. The routine NHL contract wouldn't fit the bill. Canadiens then added the astonishing five-year clause to their cash offer and Jean signed. Yes, I did tell Jean something that he undoubtedly knew himself but kept deep down—that much as he loved Quebec, if he really loved to play hockey, there was only one league in which to play and one team with which to play. Again, his idol had always been Rocket Richard and the thought of being a team mate intrigued Jean."

The background of the signing has to be considered in any analysis of the history of Canadiens not only because it was the most-discussed and longest-negotiated of any

rookie-wooing in NHL annals but also because of its
stupendous impact on hockey.

It doomed the Quebec Senior Hockey League; with
Beliveau's departure, the home crowds fell to five thousand and the away crowds fell off accordingly. The league
never did recover and, in time, faded from the scene.

As for the Canadiens, his signing started the team—to
use General Manager Selke's words—"on an era of prosperity in talent that may never again be matched."

The prophecy by Selke in October 1953 sounded then
on the exuberant, over-optimistic side. As this is written
18 years and 500 Beliveau goals and 10 Stanley Cups
later, the prophet could almost be accused of understatement.

Success Story

On the eve of the 1956 Stanley Cup playoffs, the Rangers found themselves facing a fearsome task. They had finished in third place and thus won the dubious honour of meeting the first-place Canadiens in the semi-finals. Canadiens had finished a whopping twelve games (twenty-four points) ahead of the pack, sparked by the surge of Jean Beliveau who picked up the scoring crown and the most valuable player award en route. In seventy games, he had scored or assisted in eighty-nine goals despite 143 minutes in the penalty boxes (second highest in the whole league).

Coach Phil Watson of the Rangers was asked by the New York writers if he had devised any special strategy to stop Beliveau.

"Yes, I have," replied Watson, "and after checking over the Official Rules Book, I find nothing against them."

"Them?" injected a writer.

Watson nodded: "Hand grenades."

Looking back to 1953/54 and Beliveau's full-fledged debut as an NHL toiler, there can be no doubt that he was a lucky rookie to be surrounded by such a formidable team. True, Canadiens had ended 1952/53 in second place, fifteen points behind Detroit, but they were

95

the familiar Flying Frenchmen in the playoffs, demolishing Chicago in seven harsh semi-final games and Boston Bruins (who had upset Detroit) in a five-game final for the Stanley Cup.

Canadiens' regular goaler was Gerry McNeil; his sub, Jacques Plante who was destined to win the Vezina (top goaler) Trophy six times, got into only three of the seventy scheduled games. Ahead of the cage was a rock-ribbed defence including Doug Harvey who was on his way to immortality as a seven-time winner of the Norris (top defenceman) Trophy; Butch Bouchard, a future Hockey-Hall-of-Famer; Tom Johnson, a future Norris Trophy winner, and Dollard St. Laurent.

Ahead of that defence was a whole batch of headliner names including Rocket Richard, Elmer Lach, Boom Boom Geoffrion, Bert Olmstead, Dickie Moore, Billy Reay, Ken Mosdell and Floyd Curry.

But injuries hit Canadiens' super-ballyhooed rookie severely in his baptismal season—he got into only forty-four of the seventy regular games.

The more cynical members of the Press Box began wondering early and aloud if Beliveau was actually brittle—if all is not gold that glitters in senior ranks.

So much was expected of him that the cynics failed to appreciate that even in missing more than one-third of the Canadiens' games he had participated in thirty-four goals (13-21) to tie for twenty-sixth spot in NHL scoring —ahead of such stars as Toronto's George Armstrong, Boston's Milt Schmidt and Rangers' Max Bentley.

It was also significant that under the extreme playoff pressure that followed he ended third, participating in ten goals (2-8) in ten games.

Years later, he confessed: "As long as I can remember in my hockey career, I seem to have known great pressure. Fans in Quebec remembered that when I was a junior, sometimes I would score four, five and maybe more goals in a game. The same in senior; when I would get only one goal, people would ask me on the street: 'What was the matter last night, Jean?' Then when I got up to the NHL with all that publicity, the pressure was even worse—how could I explain that it was easier to score five goals in senior hockey than one in the NHL? It would sound like an alibi."

In his second season—when the "Sophomore Jinx" so often cuts down newcomers to the Big Time—Jean zoomed to stardom. During the regular seventy-game season, he amassed thirty-seven goals and thirty-six assists. He had participated in seventy-three goals in seventy games; in the playoffs his 6-7 record saw him participate in thirteen goals in twelve games.

But for the second time in his two NHL seasons, he missed "my supreme ambition"—getting his name inscribed on the Stanley Cup. Both times Canadiens bowed out in the finals.

Then, in 1955/56, came the Beliveau blast—when he really soared to the superstar heights impatiently awaiting him. But the blast began more like a flame-out.

"I don't think I was ever so discouraged as I was at the start of the 1955/56 season," admits Beliveau. "I must have hit fifteen goal posts before coach Toe Blake told me to start shooting at the net rather than at a particular spot in the net until I broke my slump. Sure enough, a couple went in and I did all right."

The term "all right" is putting it mildly. Beliveau got inside the goal posts for forty-seven goals, assisted on forty-one others, to win the league scoring championship, the Hart (most valuable player) Trophy and followed up with tying the existing record for goals in Stanley Cup playoffs, twelve, shared jointly with Rocket Richard.

The Beliveau blast also swept Canadiens onto the glory trail for five consecutive Stanley Cup wins—a feat unequalled before or since, in the fifty-year history of the NHL.

Through that five-year span Beliveau's stature assumed

dynamic dimension. In a league where a twenty-goal
scorer is regarded as something very special, the five
scheduled seasons saw him score forty-seven, thirty-three,
twenty-seven, forty-five and thirty-four. Adding his
assists, during the span, he participated in an incredible
total of 396 points!

To which may be added a forty-one-game playoff record in the span where he participated in fifty-five goals.

Those were dazzling years for Canadiens' fans—their
vista was ablaze with spectacular stars. Just consider
those five years in terms of the All-Star teams voted
annually by panels of press, radio and TV hockey experts
in the six NHL cities:

During the span there were named five "first" All-Star
teams—a total of thirty positions. Canadien players filled
half of them.

Five "second" All-Star teams were named—again
totalling thirty positions. Canadien players filled one-third
of them.

In 1956 and 1959, four of the six-man "first" team
were Canadiens.

Plante ruled throughout the span as Vezina Trophy
goaler, highlighted by his sensational stinginess of 1955/
1956 when he gave up an average of only 1.86 goals per
game in the regular season and 1.80 in the playoffs.

There was Harvey, dominating the defencemen as best-
in-the-biz.

There was left-winger Dickie Moore who took fire after
a career showing three trips down to the minors. In
1957/58 he sharpshooted his way to the NHL scoring
championship and repeated in 1958/59. He was red hot
in the latter season's playoffs; eleven games saw him "in"
on seventeen goals.

There was still Rocket Richard—true, those five years
were his last but, typically, it was the damnedest fade-out
ever staged by any NHL performer. During that span—
so often referred to as a "sad" period for Rocket fans—

he missed through injuries a total of ninety-six regular games, the equivalent of more than one and one-third seasons, yet he participated in an astounding record of two hundred and forty goals! Of that total, he netted one hundred and twenty-two. In playoff action he scored twenty-five, assisted on nineteen.

It was a superbly balanced team with the key to championship—"strength down the middle." In that connection, what seemed at the time to be just another rugged incident, with humorous overtones, demands re-evaluation as something big in Canadiens' history. It was at the fall training camp leading into the start of that five-year span.

The Rocket's kid brother, Henri, had been given what was regarded as something of a "courtesy" tryout at training camp because of his excellent record with the Canadiens Juniors. He was only nineteen years old, only one hundred and sixty pounds, only five feet seven—everybody acknowledged the kid had oodles of spirit and drive but everybody knew he just didn't have a chance to click with the big Canadien machine—not for a while at least, if ever. The only trouble was that Henri just about took over the puck in training camp; he dominated the ice.

Then came the incident. A frantic messenger rushed up to Selke's office during a practice to pant out: "Mr. Selke, *both* Richards have been knocked unconscious!"

Selke rushed down to the physiotherapy clinic. Sure enough, the brothers had collided and, to make it more complicated, they had been playing on the same line. The collision had taken place behind the opposing net with both going all-out; nobody was quite sure which one had had the puck. The Rocket was a ten-stitch case. Standing beside the table on which his big brother lay, Henri was bleeding from a head cut and sniffing at smelling salts.

The Rocket's first words were unusually mild: "You better take care of yourself, Henri; you're liable to get hurt."

Selke walked away, deep in thought. He wasn't entirely surprised when, toward the end of the training session, the Rocket turned up at the office with young Henri who could speak no English at the time.

"Mr. Selke," said the Rocket, "my brother wants to play with Canadiens."

Selke waved them to chairs and tried to ease out of it with comment to the effect that Henri had one more year of eligibility in junior ranks and the season would round him off. Next season might—

Henri shook his head and looked right at Selke. Selke had seen that look before in young eyes and he stopped cold. He said to the Rocket:

"How much does he want?"

The Rocket repeated the question in French. Henri shrugged.

"It really doesn't matter, Mr. Selke," said the Rocket, "he just wants to play for the big team. How about two thousand dollars to sign and the usual rate for rookies, one hundred dollars a game [seven thousand dollars a season]?"

Selke paused amid conflicting thoughts—would it ruin the kid? He glanced over the desk into the blazing, eager eyes, sighed and pulled out a contract. He filled in the terms as asked. Henri was all smiles as they shook hands. But as the two brothers were leaving Selke called them back, asked for the contract and tore it up.

"I'm changing it to five thousand dollars for signing," he said. "Henri is going to make good and I don't want him to feel Canadiens have taken advantage of his youth."

They had Beliveau for first-string centre, Ralph Backstrom was coming along but who could possibly have anticipated that, within three seasons, Henri Richard would take over the first All-Star centre position and shove Beliveau to the second team? The following season saw Beliveau back on the first team but Henri was on the second.

It was unprecedented strength down the middle—all the way to perhaps the greatest goalie of all time.

Beliveau made the first team in the fifth year of the world championship span—four firsts and one second. In 1960/61 Canadiens again ended atop the league with Beliveau on the first All-Stars and Henri on the second team; but Canadiens were eliminated in the semi-finals.

They ended league champs in 1961/62 but again died in the semi-finals. The press pundits pointed out that Beliveau made neither All-Star team and added: "As Beliveau goes, so go the Canadiens." In 1962/63 they ended in third position and the wise comment looked wiser.

In the summer of 1963, Jean reached the age of thirty-two after two eighteen-goal seasons. He was weary of queries about his health, and of press conjecture; and frustrated over failing to keep up with the headlines he had been making for half his life. Finally, he came to his most momentous decision. He had been offered a major post in the huge Molson Brewery organization for whom he had been doing some publicity work.

"I have come to you for advice," Jean said to Senator Hartland de M. Molson, head man of both the brewery and the Canadiens, "on the subject of whether or not to retire. I no longer feel my work on the ice justifies my being there. What should I do? Retire and take the position offered here or try another season?"

The senator smiled across the desk. "I am not going to influence your decision, Jean. Whichever way you decide I will be lucky to have you working for me."

The sun beamed back into Jean's life. The senator's warm reply with utter lack of commiseration or diplomatic hinting about being "over the hill' was just what the doctor could have ordered. Jean didn't realize it then, or possibly hasn't realized up to now, that the senator had long before learned how to deal with courageous men who were losing their confidence—he had learned as a fighter pilot in the Battle of Britain and later as a commanding officer of young pilots in the Royal Canadian Air Force.

"I will try another season," said Jean happily.

Revived in mind, he skated through 1963/64 like a rookie, scored twenty-eight goals, assisted on fifty others, won the Hart (most valuable player) Trophy for the second time and made the second All-Stars as Canadiens ended first.

The 1964/65 season, his twelfth in the NHL, began bleakly. An injured leg sidelined him for three weeks at the start and he had only five goals, ten assists, by the halfway mark. It was late for a take-off but that's precisely what The Gentle Giant did—he came up with fifteen goals and thirteen assists in the second half, followed by one of the greatest Stanley Cup performances of all time.

Canadiens knocked off Toronto Leafs in the semi-finals and beat out Chicago Hawks in a sizzling final series that went to the full seven games. Beliveau totalled eight goals and eight assists in the thirteen playoff games; among the ten goals in which he participated in the final series was the goal at fourteen seconds of the seventh game that won the Cup. A new trophy had been established, winner to be selected by the League Governors, to be given (with a cheque for one thousand dollars) to "the most valuable player for his team in the entire playoffs." Jean was named the first winner, unanimously.

The next season, 1965/66, saw him start off just as he had ended in the spring and we of the Press Boxes found ourselves wondering aloud at the burning desire that kept this thirty-four-year-old superstar skating with rookie-like hunger for goals. He scored twenty-nine, helped set up forty-eight others. His five goals and five assists in ten playoff games contributed mightily to another Stanley

Cup win and he was barely nosed out by Detroit goalie Roger Crozier for the Smythe Trophy.

By now even the casual fans were beginning to talk about a skill that is generally obscured in the high-speed shifting of hockey attacks—namely, ice generalship. Even the coach cannot be a general once the puck is dropped; he can put lines together, order certain strategy, outline weaknesses and strengths but out on the ice there has to be an extraordinary type of athlete of whom even more is demanded than the football quarterback.

Whereas the quarterback calls plays (from a stopped position) his personal attacking demands are largely confined to throwing passes or handing off the ball to carriers via the ground route. He seldom carries. He seldom has to tackle or block. He is usually protected by massive front lines from full-force tackles.

The ice general, on the other hand, is "right in there" where the action is. He has to be a receiver as well as a giver, he is a constant target for jarring bodychecks. He is expected to be able to score and to stop the opposition from scoring. Most of his generalizing has to be "by ear" —instant action replaces football's set-up plays.

Beliveau had long since proven his ability as a scoring star but now he was making ice generalship apparent to the thousands in the rinks as well as the millions looking at television screens.

If I were asked to describe one classical example, I'd have to pick one that flashed into the final forty seconds of a game at the Montreal Forum on January 28, 1967.

Canadiens were leading the Rangers 3-2. Ranger coach Emile Francis had yanked goalie Ed Giacomin for an extra forward in a desperate effort to tie the score.

Canadiens, who should have been playing a tight defensive game, broke loose as Claude Provost snaked his way around a Ranger cover and passed recklessly to Beliveau just inside the Ranger blueline.

Beliveau . . . an empty net . . . 15,000 fans on their

feet, screaming . . . Beliveau burning with the knowledge that he was only a few goals away from his most cherished milestone—his four hundredth regular-season goal!

By the time Beliveau had gained complete control of the puck—and himself—he was a bit on the right-wing approach. Ranger All-Stars defenceman, Harry Howell, and Rod Gilbert were skating backwards ahead of him, blocking in upright position since they knew a tumbling attempt at blocking would only invite the tricky stickhandler to veer around the body, or bodies, and fire.

I happened to be on my way to the Canadiens' dressing-room at that moment, with forty seconds to go, and was directly behind the Ranger goal. There were two sets of legs and two sticks between Beliveau and the empty net but everybody in the rink was waiting breathlessly for the savage Beliveau slapshot to rip the puck through the woods and into the gaping net.

Beliveau didn't even fake a shot. He tried a deke to the right, got enmeshed with Howell, lost the puck which skimmed into a corner. Rangers regained possession and mounted one more attack as the siren sounded, ending the game.

In the dressing-room, I asked Beliveau why he hadn't shot?

"Oh, I thought of it—believe me, I thought of it," he grinned, "but they might have blocked it. The puck might have shot ahead of Howell and Gilbert, giving two All-Stars a running start for an attack, while my momentum would have taken me behind the net, out of range for any possible backchecking. With a close lead of only 3-2, one has to think of his team first, although that empty net will likely keep me awake all night."

It struck me then—I'd bet that 99.9 per cent of the viewers thought Beliveau had pulled a boner in not trying a shot and had been outwitted in an attempt to deke by a pair of All-Stars. Instead, ice-general Beliveau had been thinking one play ahead.

Unfunny Thing on Way to Forum

To most outsiders there is a magical quality about the whole Montreal hockey scene. A tradition, a heritage, a mystique remain with the team and the city even in years like this one, when the Canadiens are struggling just to stay above the .500 mark and are in imminent danger of losing the cup in the playoffs . . . . Other teams have heroes; the Canadiens have demigods, of whom the greatest was Maurice (Rocket) Richard . . . . If a number of so-so hockey players have slipped in among the gods, the heritage still lives. Surely La Belle Province *will produce yet another marvel to repel* les étrangers *and lead Montreal back to the top.* Sports Illustrated, *April 3, 1967.*

In mid-November of 1966 with an atmosphere of fiesta permeating the fiftieth anniversary season of the National Hockey League, an unfunny thing had happened on the way to the Forum. Montreal Canadiens' faithful found themselves going there to root for a last-place team.

It was, of course, utterly incredible. Prior to the season a six-city poll of NHL experts had been conducted by the *Hockey News.* The result was front-paged with a double-deck headline in red:

CANADIENS UNANIMOUSLY SELECTED
AS TEAM TO BEAT IN NEWS' POLL

The report credited Canadiens with a "first" in the seventeen-season history of the paper's annual pre-season poll. It was the first time a team had swept all first-place votes: "Winners of the Stanley Cup the past two years, Canadiens appear to be strong, if not more potent, this season and this factor obviously influenced the selectors."

Then the roof fell in.

After ten games of the new season the proud champs were down in the NHL cellar and the "I-told-you-so" crowd was sagely saying that age had finally caught up, that over-confidence had finally caught up, that the coach had finally lost his magical touch after winning seven Stanley Cups and eight league championships in eleven seasons, that there was dissension between team and general manager.

However, the players mustn't have been reading the papers. They kept on plodding through rough seas caused mainly by the jelling of a powerful Chicago Hawks machine that took them all the way to the league title. Meanwhile, New York Rangers given the monkey gland treatment by the inspirational comeback of Boom Boom Geoffrion, and Boston Bruins perked up somewhat by an astounding eighteen-year-old rookie, Bobby Orr, came up with unexpected wins and ties.

It took another month for the Canadiens to pant their way into fourth place but even that last playoff berth remained a shaky perch until the dying gasps of the season.

In addition to an upsurge in opposition, the Canadiens were harshly hit by injuries, the most serious of which were suffered by team captain Jean Beliveau, No. 1 goalie Gump Worsley and three regular defencemen.

Gump's knee injury forced him into surgery in December and when he finally got back, he reinjured the knee in the second game. The much-ballyhooed Canadien "defence wall" became as porous as a sieve with injuries to J. C. Tremblay (concussion), Terry Harper (dislocated shoulder) and Ted Harris (broken finger) while 1965/66 first All-Star defenceman, Jacques Laperrière, after missing the latter part of that season with a fractured ankle, never did recover anything like his form in 1966/67 when he also missed nine games with the walking wounded.

Offensively, chaos was caused by Beliveau's absence from a total of seventeen games (sprained thumb, a pulled muscle and an eye injury that almost ended his career). His absence caused line shuffles with the shuffles being re-shuffled due to the various absences caused by injuries to Henri Richard, Claude Provost, Gilles Tremblay, Dick Duff and Bobby Rousseau.

Actually, every single player on the Canadiens roster was injured at some time during the season. Club physiotherapist, Yvon Belanger, reported a total of more than five hundred treatments were given to the walking-wounded and tenderly-toted cases.

"Since I entered this league as a player thirty-one years ago," moaned coach Blake, "I've never known anything like it."

The moan recalled an editorial in the New York *Sun* commenting with startled awe on the invasion of "Canada's game" in Manhattan in 1925. It said in part:

Hockey is a combination of football, golf, soccer, prize-fighting, tong war and the last riot of Herrin, Illinois. It is a crime wave on ice.

Sporting enthusiasts who like their thrills served fresh every second and who consider any sport dull when any of the contestants are in an upright position have found what they ordered. Here, at last, is a game played while every contestant is in the act of falling through space.

It makes baseball seem like casual exercise prescribed by the doctor for old gentlemen with stiff joints. Beside it football looks like something they bring into the nursery to keep the children out of mischief.

When it is time for a hockey game to begin the

referee skates to the centre of the rink and blows a whistle. This is a signal to all physicians, nurses and internes to get ready for business. He then drops the rubber heel and flees for his life. The rubber heel is immediately battled for by the opposing teams on the theory of an eye for an eye, a tooth for a tooth and a fracture for a try at the goal cage. During the carnage the busiest individual in the arena is the goal-tender, who is dressed like the man in the Michelin tire advertisement, and who has to stop more missiles than the City of Rheims stopped German shells.

After the end of the final period surgeons examine the goal-tenders. The game is awarded to the side whose goal-tender has the best chance of recovery.

However, in the spring of 1967, one of the oldest axioms in sport was proven anew—the one about sticking with the champion until he is beaten.

Canadiens surged in the stretch drive of the regular schedule; in the last sixteen games they won ten and tied five. They cinched second place on the last night of the schedule.

The semi-finals thus saw them face New York Rangers while Chicago Hawks, first-place finishers, took on the third-place Toronto Leafs.

Rangers, in the playoffs for the first time in five seasons, looked like world-beaters in the opening game with a 4-1 lead and eleven minutes left to play. From the press box we could see hundreds of fans making for the exits to get a jump on the traffic. They must have received a jolting shock on reading the sport pages next morning.

It appears that the only ones in the Forum who felt Canadiens weren't beaten were the Canadiens themselves. Within the span of one minute and fifty-one seconds, they rattled in three goals to tie the score, went ahead less than two minutes later and ended up, 6-4.

From that whirlwind finish Canadiens retained their momentum, sweeping the series with four straight wins.

It sounds as though Rangers folded but actually they didn't—they were simply beaten four times and certainly were not out-fought. After the final game in Madison Square Garden when Rangers out-shot the Flying Frenchmen, 34-29, only to lose after six minutes of overtime, the usually biased fans gave both teams a standing ovation—a fitting and sporty farewell, indeed, to playoff hockey in the about-to-be-demolished Garden.

And, for the twenty-second time in 50 NHL springs, Canadiens entered the Stanley Cup finals.

But then they ran headlong into a buzz-saw.

The Toronto Leafs, who had ended the regular schedule nineteen points (almost ten games) behind the highly favoured Chicago Hawks, scored the upset of the season by skating and bumping their way over the scalped Hawks in six games.

The Canadiens-Leafs series has to go down as one of the most spectacular, up-and-down classic clashes of Stanley Cup history.

It opened with a wild, 6-2 romp as Canadiens literally skated Leafs into the Forum ice. Then, while fans in both cities were agreed for once that it looked like another four-straight sweep for Canadiens, the Leafs took another deep swig of the heady upset wine and shocked the reigning world champs with a 3-0 shutout win.

The series shifted to Toronto. Game No. 3 opened at eight P.M. and ended at seven minutes before midnight as Leafs' Bobby Pulford potted the 3-2 sudden-death winner after the most fantastically, free-wheeling overtime in the memory of the press box. Both sides almost entirely abandoned defensive hockey and went for broke until one puck finally went in. It was the second-longest overtime in Maple Leaf Gardens' history.

Game No. 4, still playing on Toronto ice, saw Canadiens overwhelm the Leafs and awe the home fans with another 6-2 crusher to even things at two wins apiece in the best-of-seven series—and the next game back on Montreal Forum ice.

Leafs took the fifth and sixth games, 4-1 and 3-1, although Canadiens out-shot them 38-29 and 41-36. Leafs' upset ways had gone all the way to the 1967 Stanley Cup on wings of a puck-stopping flight into the very select stratosphere reserved for goalies who are good—not just lucky. Terry Sawchuk who had been the goat of both 6-2 Leaf losses was the hero of the two big wins in the final games. Johnny Bower who had come up with the shutout and the overtime win was sidelined with a pulled thigh muscle in the pregame warm-up of the fourth game.

A total of 381 shots had been fired by both teams in the six games with Canadiens out-shooting Leafs by an unbelievable margin of thirty-one shots—only to lose by an aggregate of seventeen goals to sixteen.

Hockey seems to have a hold on its players that no other game quite equals—oldtimers just don't want to leave the game and this saga of the padded ancients was a memorable case in point.

Bower was well into his forty-third year of life and his twenty-second year in pro hockey (minor as well as major). Sawchuk in his thirty-eighth year had also spent more than half his life, twenty years, in pro hockey (minor and major). They were aided by some of the most furious and sustained forechecking and backchecking by their mates in the annals of Stanley Cup hockey. Although the speed-emphasizing Canadiens out-shot Leafs in five of the six games, the relentless Leaf checking diminished the force and accuracy of many Canadien shots by forcing the attackers to hurry up those shots or to fire from bad angles.

On the calm morrow as the storm battle gave way to the sombre serenity of a champagne hangover, the new champions admitted the series had been the harshest fight of their hockey lives.

For the old champions, it was a depressing morrow— gone was the elation in knowing they had come all the way from last place through a casualty-strewn campaign of unprecedented dimension to the Stanley Cup finals. The feel of the true champion had carried them to what, in many ways, was their finest season.

Beliveau again emerged as the top Canadien playoff scorer with six goals, five assists in 10 games. Based on points per playoff game, he thus won recognition as hockey's all-time top Stanley Cup scorer with an average of 1.09 points in 118 games. (Gordie Howe was second with 1.04 in 150 games, followed by other ex-Canadiens, Rocket Richard and Boom-Boom Geoffrion.)

Across the nation from some seven million living-room fans who followed the series via television, came plaudits for what was generally hailed as a superbly thrilling Canadian Centennial Year gift in the form of an all-Canadian final series played in the game's most hectic, two-way tradition. But the dejected Canadiens were more conscious of their failure to keep a promise made three springs ago.

The promise had been made during an exultant party thrown by Montreal's Mayor Jean Drapeau at the Chalet atop Mount Royal following Canadiens' 1964/65 sweep to the Stanley Cup. It was a wingding banquet with coach Toe Blake, bolstered by bouquets and bubbly, replying to the dynamic mayor's tribute with:

"Your Worship, we will not only win the Cup again in 1966 but, specially for you and the opening of your Expo 67, we'll win it still again in 1967!"

It had seemed to be a wild promise at the time but the fabulous Flying Frenchmen came through with a repeat Cup win in 1966 and ended 1967 within one game of fulfilling the pledge.

At Expo 67, Mayor Drapeau took time off from entertaining Hailie Selassie and Ed Sullivan to tell the world:

"Les Canadiens gave it a good try—they have merely stepped out of the throne room for a breath of air."

The season that left Montreal limp had rounded out a remarkable quarter-century of NHL hockey for the local fans. In the twenty-five completed seasons of the six-team league up to the expansion era, Canadiens had won the league championship twelve times and the Stanley Cup ten times. They had ended second eight times and out of the playoffs only once.

Reviewers of the NHL half-century mused over an oddity. Since fickle Lady Luck never seems to linger with a single lover in sport for so long a span, just what was the secret of Canadiens' success? The obvious answer in a single sentence is: Canadiens have had good teams and good coaches. But it's not that simple; for long-range success the basic reason has to lie in the front office.

The obvious answer in a single sentence is: Canadiens have had good teams and good coaches. But it's not that simple; for long-range success the basic reason has to lie in the front office.

Agreed, neither the president nor the general manager nor any other front office staffers score any goals. The coach is closer to the scoring in that he puts together the lines, outlines strategy and keeps the team a team— but he doesn't actually score any goals either. For the scoring of goals and the prevention of goals-against, it's strictly a matter of players and enough good players to have bench depth. In these days of rapid on-the-fly changes, one's so-called "third line" often find themselves tangling with the other team's "first line." If you haven't got the calibre in depth, you just can't win championships.

Getting a championship supply of that calibre while

keeping a crop for the future growing down on the farm calls for more than mere money. If somebody ever gets around to doing a Broadway play on the Canadiens, it could be called *How to Succeed in Hockey by Really Trying,* as was illustrated in dramatic fashion by their fourth goaler of the 1966/67 season.

Charlie Hodge had been in for twenty-seven games, had a smart goals-against average of 2.60 but the team wasn't scoring and wasn't winning. Gump was lost to the surgeons and the natives in the Canadien front office were getting restless. A replacement goalie for Gump was brought up, Gary Bauman, but he injured his back after two games. In mid-February, with Gump Worsley again injured, General Manager Sam Pollock announced that a fourth goaler would be put into action, Rogatien Vachon from Palmarolle.

Who? From where?

Even the veteran press-boxers were asking one another questions. We finally got some vital statistics: twenty-one years old, five feet seven, one hundred and fifty-five pounds, born in the Quebec whistle stop called Palmarolle he had been stopping pucks the previous season for the Junior "A" Thetford Mines (Que.) Canadiens before turning pro with the club's Central Professional League team at Houston, Texas, in 1966/67. He had appeared in action at the Hull training camp of the NHL Canadiens but the writers had concentrated on the Montreal camp where the big team worked out.

Anyway, even if the wee goalie with penetrating eyes and wandering ways around the goal area had been at the Montreal camp, he wouldn't have received any special attention from us. He would have been lost in the mob scene.

The many called for the few to be chosen established a record for any club's September camp in NHL history, and of the one hundred and ten players present thirteen were goalkeepers. And why should we watch a junior-calibre rookie puck-stopper while Canadiens still had the Worsley-Hodge combine, current holders of the Vezina Trophy?

However, somebody up there—up in the Canadiens' front office—had been watching, and a detailed report on Vachon had enough beef in it to give the kid a contract at Houston. The report did point out that Vachon was inclined to leave his net too often and too far. This wandering is thrilling stuff for the fans but two great goalers, Jacques Plante and Eddie Giacomin, had found the price too high.

Wandering by goalies is dangerous not only because of the bodycheck menace (once beyond their goal crease, goalies become targets the same as other players). They are a rugged and daring breed who face a surprising amount of physical contact as it is and their extra padding makes them fairly formidable in terms of absorbing bumps. But, in the course of dashing out, dashing back and wheeling into position for a save; they have to take their eyes off the puck and, in the NHL where shooters get their shots away in a blur of slapping motion, the wandering goalie often isn't set for an immediate save. If his weight is on the wrong skate, he's had it.

The fault could be corrected by direct coaching orders. On the other hand, the report on Vachon stressed his nimbleness not only atop skates but with his hands— particularly his left, and glove, hand. There was something unusual noted in that Vachon, a natural southpaw, held his stick in his right—and weaker—hand. Thus his stronger hand was free for puck-snaring. In this regard, the lad is probably unique among NHL goalers of all time.

Finally, it was noted that the kid had an eager flair about him that often sparked jaded teams. A skilled goaler who makes hard shots look easy doesn't do nearly so much for a jaded or depressed team as one who makes easy shots look hard.

Early in 1967, General Manager Sam Pollock took a trip down to Houston to see if there was anything there to pump a little adrenalin into the listless parent team up north. He didn't go down particularly to see Rogatien, but that night Rogatien made Sam's eyes pop with fifty stops that had the rink in an uproar.

"I think we should give the kid a try at the nets," he told coach Blake in February, "what have we got to lose?"

Vachon made his NHL debut at the Forum and whether or not the Canadiens were due to take fire anyway will always be a debating point. But the fact is that, during the team's blistering stretch drive, Vachon was in nineteen games and the Canadiens won twelve, tied four, lost only three. In 1,137 minutes of facing the opposing NHL sharpshooters he allowed only forty-seven goals to get by for a lowly 2.48 per game average. He registered a shutout. He even entered the league scoring lists with one point for an assist.

In the press box, we began recalling the tradition of goalkeeping greatness that has almost continuously been a hallmark of Canadien teams from Georges Vezina on. The trophy named in his memory for annual award to the least-scored-against regular goalie has been presented forty times with Canadien stoppers winning it seventeen times. Jacques Plante and Bill Durnan tied for a record six-wins apiece but this Rogatien Vachon had a quality reminiscent of the first one to win it, namely, George Hainsworth, who kept it for three consecutive seasons while writing an unprecedented chapter in the annals of major league goalkeeping.

Vachon got us thinking after his first experience against the savagery of Chicago Black Hawk Bobby Hull's slapshot. When asked for his reaction, the rookie calmly shrugged: "A puck coming at you looks just the same here as back in Thetford Mines."

Vezina had been ice-water personified in the nets. After his death in the spring of 1926, Manager Leo Dandurand had bewildered Montreal fans by reaching for Hainsworth, then with Saskatoon Sheiks of the old Western Canada League. Toronto-born, Hainsworth had been a rather mature amateur playing at Kitchener, Ont., when he was turned pro by Newsy Lalonde—the ex-Canadien great then coaching the Sheiks. When Dandurand imported Hainsworth, Montreal fans in the Forum reaches gazed cynically upon a thirty-three-year-old rookie!

But the cynicism soon evaporated as Hainsworth, in his first Vezina Trophy-winning season, 1926/27, allowed only sixty-seven goals in forty-four games. The next season he allowed forty-eight in forty-four games. The third season he set a record that will never be equalled in this era of the slapshot, deflected shot and free-wheeling forward passing; he racked up an unbelievable twenty-two shutouts in forty-four games while allowing only forty-three goals.

It was much too early after Rogatien Vachon's brief, late-season appearance in 1966/67 to compare him seriously with the immortal Hainsworth, but they did match up in terms of smallness, ability to stop pucks— and coolness under a rubber barrage.

The most impressive angle of this "unknown" Vachon was that Canadiens did come up with him—just when a spark was needed.

His dramatic entry also prompted people to take a long look at the players in civilian clothes as the team went into the playoffs—the "taxi squad" who formed the excess personnel over the eighteen players allowed in uniform per game. Any of the five would have been grabbed by at least three of the other NHL teams if put up for sale.

Such depth doesn't "just happen."

For instance, during the massive '66 training camp with one hundred and ten eager beavers straining to please, General Manager Pollock explained: "We want to take a good look at the largest number of players possible in preparation for the NHL expansion a season away."

After ten days the one hundred and ten were distributed to Canadiens and their affiliated clubs, which included Quebec Aces, Cleveland Barons and Providence Reds of the American Hockey League; Seattle Totems of the Western Hockey League; Houston Apollos of the Central Professional Hockey League, and Muskegon Mohawks of the International Hockey League.

Aside from the goalers who, of course, have their own specialized qualifications to meet, there is one basic qualification for all potential Canadiens and it represents a vital part of the Canadiens' secret of success.

President David Molson explains: "Often I ask about a certain player only to have Pollock reply, 'Dave, he can't skate.' That ends it. The club's reputation for playing fire-wagon hockey—where it matters not if five goals are scored against as long as we get six—has become a tradition. Blake, as a player on the storied line with Elmer Lach and Rocket Richard, was a spectacular example of glamour in playing hockey that way and he still thinks that way. A coach can teach anything else, but a player who can't skate is a minor leaguer with us."

From the one hundred and ten who appeared at the training camps, the Canadien brass decided there were twenty-five of NHL calibre. Molson continues:

"But we were even more interested in the next twenty-five or thirty, the ones who might be regarded as 'indispensable' in June, 1967, at the first universal draft of the NHL expansion era."

Canadiens have always believed that it's important to keep the jobs of general manager and coach separate because they feel the two jobs could conflict in terms of

long-range planning. Other teams don't think that way
but Canadiens feel a coach, to be a good coach, must
be extremely close to his players. Coach Toe Blake
proved a stand-out example of how that thinking works.
At dressing-room meetings, even the trainer was ex-
cluded—what went on in the room stayed there. I have
heard Blake blasting the team but never a player. And
the players respect him not only because he has guided
them to seven Stanley Cups but also because he was a
thirteen-season player of NHL star status (with Canadiens and the old Montreal Maroons). There was built
up an unusually close liaison; Blake became one of the
team rather than the boss.

But Blake would have been less than an ordinary
human if this liaison had not made for sentiment and
loyalty toward players who had given their best in the
past and who might now be slipping. It might also have
been nearly impossible for Blake to be coldly objective
about a young player who was really trying—but whose
effort was just short.

So Blake's job was established—to coach and win.

I have often heard the team criticized for "lack of
sportsmanship", for being "lousy losers", but I have
played against handball opponents so anxious to say,
"Good shot!", that they failed to make a desperation
recovery of that shot. On the other hand, I played handball against Rocket Richard and he'd dive into the floor
at a shot two inches above the floor—seemingly impossible to recover but at least he'd try. I see, in that feverish
urge to win, protection for the Canadien fans who pay
their money to see a team giving every last ounce.
Almost twenty consecutive years of sellouts at the Forum
have repaid that utter honesty of action.

Perhaps the difference between the amateur and professional approach is best exemplified by an amusing
incident that followed my return in mid-December of

1956 from the sunny "down under" of the world. I had been covering the Summer Olympics in Australia and was sporting a mahogany tan a kindly editor allowed me to pick up on the beaches of Hawaii on the way home. Now I was in the Canadiens' dressing room enjoying the envy of the hockey palefaces.

They pressed me about the big show of amateurism. Boom Boom Geoffrion commented: "Canada didn't do so well, eh?"

"No-o-o," I agreed, "we ended down in points—sixteenth to be exact among the nations—but ..." I added with a flourish, "as Baron de Coubertin, founder of the modern Olympics, used to remind us: 'It's not who wins but how you play the game!' "

There was a thoughtful silence in the Canadiens' dressing room—but only for a few moments. Rocket Richard snorted:

"That Frenchman sounds like a born loser."

I am not recommending that attitude to kids in sport, but if I am going to recommend a spectacle for readers with a few hard-earned dollars to invest, I feel the win-or-else Canadiens always make the investment worthwhile.

When Sam Pollock took over as general manager— Blake's immediate boss—we of the press expected fireworks because both Sam and Toe were opinionated and, at times, downright stubborn. But it proved an amazing marriage. Blake kept right on handling the team and never even knowing what each player was being paid; Pollock made the personnel decisions. If they had heated arguments we never heard about it. But I doubt if they disagreed much because each recognized in the other that restless urge to win in no-holds-barred action.

Pollock, at the end of 1966/67, concluded his third season as general manager at the age of 41. For ten years before that he was the man largely responsible for keeping Canadiens' powerful farm system in high gear. As Director of Farm Personnel for the club, it was his task to stock the entire farm system with the best talent he could find and sign. When the Eastern Professional Hockey League was formed in 1959/60, Pollock was named General Manager of the Hull-Canadiens and retained that position during the four-year history of the league. His actual playing experience was limited to a few seasons in the minors before he turned to coaching Montreal's junior Canadiens whom he piloted to the Memorial (junior) Cup championship in 1949/50. After the team was moved to become the Hull-Canadiens (before turning pro en masse in the EPHL) he again won the Memorial in 1957/58. When Canadiens decided to enter a team in the new Central Pro League at Omaha (before shifting to Houston) he put together a roster that won the league title in 1963/64.

Pollock has been tagged a "cold-fish executive" which President Molson shrugs off:

"Sam wasn't appointed to win popularity contests, but his popularity will suffer only with the players who aren't producing. And I can't imagine Montreal fans, the keenest in hockey, being irked at that."

Pollock took over the G.M. reins from one of the wisest front office minds in the history of hockey, Frank J. Selke sr., who retired at the conclusion of the 1963/64 season. Selke had left Toronto Leafs to succeed Tommy Gorman whose managerial record included seven Stanley Cup teams with three different clubs—Ottawa Senators twice, Chicago Black Hawks and Montreal Maroons in successive years (coaching both teams as well) and twice with Canadiens.

In his own headline-haunting way, Tommy was quite incomparable but he had little patience with farm produce. His interest was concentrated on proven talent. Under him Canadiens' Cup win in 1944 was their first in thirteen years but when Selke inherited the first-place,

Cup-holding team in the summer of 1946, he warned the club president, Senator Donat Raymond, that with prosperity coming from around the corner, cash offers to other clubs would lose their allure: Canadiens just had to bolster their feeble farm system and begin growing their own talent crops.

His prediction came true two seasons later when Canadiens ended out of the playoffs; that was in 1947/48. It was Selke who brought Pollock closer to the front office together with former defence star, Kenny Reardon. The three would discuss all moves before Selke made a decision. From it all grew a strong foundation at the junior affiliation level. Bernie (Boom Boom) Geoffrion came along. Dickie Moore. Henri Richard. André Pronovost. Don Marshall. Claude Provost. Bob Turner. It was Selke himself who spotted a defenceman on the Winnipeg Monarchs who had been overlooked but eventually won the Norris Trophy as hockey's greatest defenceman (1959), Tom Johnson, currently coach of the Boston Bruins. When a kid named Jean Beliveau was wooed away from the Canadien chain, Selke got him back. As the aging stars faded, there always seemed to be—and still are—new faces with bodies attached that amaze. Like rookie Rogatien Vachon.

Senator Raymond turned down repeated offers for his beloved Canadiens, seeking new owners "worthy of a great hockey heritage." He was openly elated in 1953 to turn over controlling interest (including the Forum) to the highly respected Molson family, whose history extends farther back than that of Montreal.

There was a lot of money involved but, naive as it sounds, we who were close to the transaction knew the financial aspect was secondary. Senator Raymond certainly had no need of another four million dollars while the Forum-with-Canadiens merged into the Molson Family enterprises of which the brewery and extensive real estate holdings represented only a part. The family has long been involved actively in community service activities, such as hospitals and schools, at the administrative level.

Senator Hartland Molson stated in announcing the huge deal:

"We don't own the team really. The public of Montreal, in fact the entire Province of Quebec owns the Canadiens. The club is more than a professional sports organization. It is an institution, a way of life."

In 1964 the senator found his many enterprises, as well as sessions at the Senate in Ottawa, prevented him from devoting as much time to hockey as he felt was required and he stepped up to the quieter seat of Chairman of the Board, passing on the presidential command to his cousin, J. David Molson, then only thirty-six. David was already a vice-president and director of the Canadian Arena Company. He had already shown executive ability in the commercial field; he soon established himself as a keen hockey mind as well. After the hockey world was bombshelled by the announcement of the dramatic NHL plan to expand itself from six to twelve cities, word got out that young Molson was one of the designers—President Bill Jennings of the New York Rangers was the other.

Undoubtedly the most intimately involved president of any NHL club, David Molson if he isn't upstairs doing what people in the front office do, can be found down on the ice with a group of friends chasing a puck. He never quite got over the fun of it during school days. When an interviewer asked him if it was true that the Molsons had bought the Forum because they were unable to get seats otherwise (the Forum has been sold out for Canadien home games for twenty years), David denied the rumour.

"The truth is," he dead-panned, "that the family wanted to make sure I had a rink to work out on."

In the professional sports world it is more than

unusual to find promoters with an almost casual regard for profits. He says:

"We (Molson and Pollock) took over a great hockey team and our only instructions were to keep it that way."

The word "only" seemed to brush aside any suggestion of holding on to a fat portion of the monies that keep pouring into the Forum box office. Of course, running a continuing champion-contender hockey franchise at the NHL level is profit-consuming. It calls for expensive players and expensive executive all the way down through the farm and scouting systems. Thirty-five road trips cost a fortune. And have you checked on the prices of hockey equipment lately? But I was most impressed in September of 1966 to note that every member of the Canadiens signed a contract on his first talk with Pollock although some of the demands must have been stiff— after all, most of the players interviewed had helped win two consecutive world championships while many had shared in acquiring eight league titles.

I asked what the secret of the meek signers was.

"We believe that those who produce success should share in it," replied President Molson. "Accordingly, our contracts offer added incentive clauses that are actually a challenge to their sportsmanship.

"We say to a player that we feel he is worth a certain number of dollars plus the chance to make an additional amount if he produces. We don't hesitate to offer contracts of up to three years where we feel it would be mutually beneficial.

"Furthermore, our policy places considerable importance on the relationship between management and players. We give them counsel on how to invest their money. We have straightened out players who have gone into debt."

Canadiens also operate as a year-round business. Printed suggestions on how to keep in shape, what specific exercises will benefit hockey muscles during the summer months, are issued at the end of each season. I can think of a few players who have been known to put on a lot of weight in the off-season; they have to report regularly for checks. It's pointed out that staying in top shape is good for them financially, while letting themselves get out of shape might hurt their team mates' chances of earning added incentive revenue. It is astonishing to see the first weight chart posted after training camp opens—few pounds separate current weight from that of the previous spring.

Staying up top or near the top doesn't just happen; it has to be made happen in major sport. This was illustrated by the way Canadiens responded to Mayor Drapeau's teasing prediction after they had failed by a whisker to deliver the Cup as promised for his Expo 67 festivities: "They have merely stepped from the throne room for a breath of air."

The expansion era had dawned. With astounding daring, the NHL doubled itself from six to twelve teams by adding California Seals, Los Angeles Kings, Minnesota North Stars, Philadelphia Flyers, Pittsburgh Penguins and St. Louis Blues. (Midway through the first season the California Seals changed their name to Oakland Seals.)

Canadiens reacted to the historic first season of expansion by completely dominating the Big Time—ending the regular schedule atop the East Division and then proving unstoppable in the playoffs by knocking off Boston Bruins in four straight games, Chicago Black Hawks in five and finally the St. Louis Blues, best of the West, four-straight.

The momentum carried them clean through the second expansion season—again they topped the East and, in the 1969 playoffs, swept through New York Rangers four-straight, the Boston Bruins in six and the St. Louis Blues four-straight.

(Whenever a playoff series goes to the seven-game

limit, as in 1971, I have wise guys smirk at me: "The teams are making some extra dough, eh?" The Canadiens of 1968 and 1969 playoff periods answered the wise guys for keeps by trimming 42 games to 27— eliminating 15 capacity crowds.)

Canadiens' re-entry into the NHL throne room in the spring of 1968 showed the results of some slick strategy at the first expansion draft in June, 1967. Somehow, the replacements forced into the team by draft losses left them with a better team in terms of balance. Although the team failed to place a single player among the top ten scorers in the regular season, Canadiens featured a stretch of 16 games without defeat—including a 12-game winning streak.

Aside from balance up front, new vigor had been added to the rearguard.

They let goaler Charlie Hodge go in the draft to the Seals and stuck with the Worsley-Vachon combo who went right on to win the Vezina Trophy. They let veteran defenceman Jean Guy Talbot go in the draft to Minnesota and brought up Serge Savard from Houston—the 21-year-old 200-pounder was due to come up anyway as the starry-eyed winner of the Central Hockey League's rookie-of-the-year award. There were other changes, minor, but contributing to spots of balance in the already strong lineup.

Typically Canadien was the between-seasons change of coach in 1968.

Hall-of-Famer Toe Blake had decided the time had come to ease the tension stretching back over 13 seasons as a player in the NHL and a coaching record of eight Canadien Stanley Cup wins. He had personally scored two Stanley Cup winning goals in his playing days, a record equalled by team mate Jean Beliveau and (in 1971) Henri Richard. He accepted the team post of assistant vice-president.

In Toe's storied shoes was placed Claude Ruel, at age

30 the youngest ever to coach in the NHL. He had been in the organization since he was fifteen as a player with Junior Canadiens. His playing career ended in 1957 when a high stick cost him the sight of his left eye. But five years as coach of the Junior Canadiens, two years as chief scout and two years as director of player development had—in the club management's opinion—prepared him to take over Blake's job.

Although Ruel was younger than some of his star players, the rookie coach took Canadiens all the way—to top the East and win 12 of 14 playoff games for the Cup.

His 1968-69 debut squad hadn't undergone any startling changes from the championship array he had inherited, but several of the players had come up with spectacularly improved performances. For instance, Yvan Cournoyer and Jean Beliveau had both blasted their way into the Top Ten Scorers, while Jacques Lemaire increased his scoring points from 42 to 63. And defenceman Serge Savard had blossomed in only his second NHL season to win the Conn Smythe Trophy as the top player in the playoffs.

The top thrill, however, had to be the one that added to the legend of "Mr. Everything". It was the goal scored by Jean Beliveau at 12.15 a.m. of April 25, 1969, four and one-quarter hours after the playoff game had started at the Forum. It eliminated Boston from the semi-finals and was rated by Red Sullivan, the former New York Rangers' player and coach, as "the greatest hockey game ever played."

Beliveau told me afterwards that he had "given up" on the particular attack and had turned to return to the Canadien zone, but "somehow Claude (Provost) recovered the puck over at the boards and whipped a bullet pass at me. I was sideways to it when the puck came and the Boston goal behind me but, from the side of my eye, I spotted an opening in the upper right corner left by the crouching goaler (Gerry Cheevers). I didn't wait to turn because that would give Cheevers a chance to line me up; I backhanded as hard as I could. I have to admit I was surprised as anybody when the puck found the opening. . . ."

Surprised? Can fire-wagon hockey produce anything but surprises? Anyway, try to beat an NHL goalie that way sometime and you'll discover there had to be a lot more than luck, especially since the puck left a curved stick—curved against a backhanded shot!

The 1969 Stanley Cup party at the Queen Elizabeth Hotel in Montreal was a swinging wingding with the whole team trying to outdo each other dancing the Frug —a muscular effort recently popularized by Prime Minister Trudeau. Even rotund Coach Claude Ruel was beaming—the players had given him a horse (no fooling!) because his only hobby was the trotters. I recall gazing over the star-studded players and their youngest-ever coach and thinking: "They've won the Stanley Cup in four of their last five seasons. How long will this dynasty last?"

The question, on looking back, is even more logical from hindsight because the stand-by Canadien goalie in the playoffs—the No. 3 goalie who never got out of civvies—was a lad named Tony Esposito. He was then only one month away from being drafted by Chicago Black Hawks into NHL immortality as the Vezina and Calder (rookie of the year) Awards winner, setting a modern record en route with 15 shutouts. What team ever had such goalkeeping depth? That, plus depth in defence and forward departments.

If my musing at that moment had been interrupted by somebody slipping into the next chair at my table— some monied and misled fellow—offering to wager that this team would end the next season in fifth place, completely out of the playoffs for the first time in twenty-two years, what odds would I have given?

I would have given at least ten-to-one odds, because there was no way—no, no way—it could happen in the still-new expansion era with so many watered-down birds to pluck.

But I could have lost my shirt.

A Wonderful, Whacky Win

When, almost on the eve of the 1971 playoffs, Canadiens' fans got their first look at the six-foot-four goaler extraordinary, Ken Dryden, those seated near his net just before a game's start noted that he closed his eyes and bowed his head. Was he praying? Or, in keeping with his reputation for relaxing, was he dozing? Finally, this author asked about it. "I do neither," said Dryden, "it's simply because I don't want to see the red lights behind the goals go on when the referee signals for testing just before dropping the puck. Whenever I've seen them flash I've had a bad game—some guys are bothered by black cats crossing their trail, with me it's red lights." He paused thoughtfully before adding, "But curiously, after the game starts, I take particular delight out of seeing a red light—at the far end of the rink."

Actually, the build-up to Canadiens' wonderful, whacky win of 1971 began with the shock of being nosed out of the 1970 playoffs. There they were, the reigning champions of hockeydom, reduced to the role of spectators at playoffs for the first time in more than two decades—missing by a meagre margin of two goals, true, but in fifth place just the same.

What happened?

Primarily, the complacency bug had bitten after two

consecutive Cups. Said defenceman Ted Harris: "So many times this season we said, next game, next game. Then there were no more games. . . ."

Henri Richard postscripted: "If a team can't make it in 75 games why should we expect somebody else to do it for us in the 76th?"

Canadiens just weren't ready for the whirlwind finish; the East Division's fourth berth was decided only in the last period of the last game—and by goals, since Rangers and Canadiens were tied in games won, lost and tied. So the deciding factor was "goals for" which accounted for Henri Richard's comment. Rangers had a two-goal edge.

Rangers made it through a 9–5 win over Detroit. Roger Crozier had been pasted with a record 65 shots in the Detroit goal, which caused his team mates to be fingered for non-effort by a number of critics in the Montreal area. But the fact was that Detroit Red Wings had entered the game with nothing to gain, while the Rangers were skating for their lives. Richard was closer to the truth.

The ulcer finish on April 5, 1970, caused all leaves to be cancelled in the Forum front office, and the feeling of frenzied effort to dam the dike extended through the summer and the entire 1970-71 campaign, which was best summarized by a Chicago writer who said to me:

"If I had made up what has happened this season in the Canadiens' camp and sent it in as a fiction book no editor would have accepted it—too implausible."

The unbelievable climax overshadowed so many weird happenings during the regular season that it's simpler to ponder over the nine-month trek to the Cup in chronological form:

Sept. 10—Ralph Backstrom, a 214-goal Canadien, fails to report to training camp, says he is unsure of whether or not to retire.

Sept. 11—Backstrom reverses the headlines of the previous day and decides to give it another go.

Oct. 6—Team stalwart and "policeman" John Ferguson decides to retire "for business reasons" four days before the season opener.

Oct. 10—Backstrom fails to show for the plane to Philadelphia and announces his retirement: "My wife and I would like to move to a warmer climate."

Oct. 17—Canadiens win their fourth consecutive game, beating Chicago 6–2, and the fans begin figuring the retirements haven't been so crippling after all. The streak ends the next night in New York; they get beat, 1–0.

Oct. 31—Defenceman Jacques Laperriere is checked into the boards by Vancouver's Orland Kurtenbach and suffers a neck injury that removes him from the lineup indefinitely.

Nov. 4—Coach Claude Ruel causes wide discussion by leaving the bench with 10 seconds to go as Canadiens barely eke out a 4–3 win at Minnesota; the pressure had gotten to him.

Nov. 7-8—Canadiens were higher than their plane after whomping Buffalo Sabres 11–2 in the two teams' first clash at the Forum on Saturday night, but were shot down in flames, 6–1, at Boston on Sunday.

Nov. 14—John Ferguson changes his mind, admits he'd like to return. Sam Pollock says he is glad.

Nov. 17—Ferguson comes back, gets standing ovation at Forum.

Nov. 29—Earlier in the month Canadiens came out of a four-game road trip with only two points. Now, a loss at Detroit makes it three out of four and question marks begin flashing over Coach Ruel's head.

Dec. 3—In an emotional press conference, Sam Pollock announces Ruel's resignation and Ruel declares he had to talk assistant Al McNeil out of quitting with him.

McNeil accepts the job. Meanwhile, skating alone down on the Forum ice, is Backstrom; he has decided to make a comeback.

Dec. 9—Canadiens suffer a 4–0 loss at Toronto before starting a string of five wins, four ties and one loss.

Jan. 1—Canadiens are in third place but the outlook isn't at all bright with Boston 17 points ahead and New York 16 points. Trade rumors mingle with New Year resolutions.

Jan. 13—The impossible happens; Canadiens en route to Minnesota announce a breathtaking trade acquisition. Frank Mahovlich, the 400-goal superstar, is obtained from Detroit—for Mickey Redmond, Bill Collins and Guy Charron.

Jan. 14—In his first game as a Canadien, Frank Mahovlich scores to salvage a 3–3 tie at Minnesota.

Jan. 27—Backstrom finally gets his wish for a warmer climate; he is traded to Los Angeles for Gordon Laboissiere who winds up in Minnesota.

Jan. 30—Serge Savard, just showing signs of old form after a leg fracture the previous March, takes a hard check from Toronto's Bobby Baun. Same leg broken, out for season.

Feb. 6—Canadiens, showing signs of jelling under Mac-Neil, meet rude jolt from Los Angeles, 6–3. Backstrom scored twice for L.A.

Feb. 11—Forum looks like New Year's Eve used to look like on Times Square as Jean Beliveau hits 500th goal stratosphere with a hat-trick in 6–2 win over Minnesota.

Feb. 27—Rogatien Vachon in great goaling form as Canadiens run streak to eight wins and a tie, but the hottest club in the league is still far off the Bruins. The second-place Rangers are their target.

March 3—A 3–0 loss to Pittsburgh jolts second-place hoping.

March 14—At Pittsburgh, Canadiens decide to try out

their latest goaling acquisition, Ken Dryden. He stars
in 5–1 win.

March 16—Another setback; Canadiens suffer their first
loss at St. Louis in four seasons, 6–2.

March 20—The Dryden brothers make NHL history as
the first goaling brother act to face one another. Ken
of Canadiens tops Dave of Buffalo, 5–2.

March 21—Ken Dryden shines as Canadiens blast
Rangers 6–2 in New York.

March 24—Jean Beliveau Night is truly one to remember; the fans donated $155,855 for his Foundation
Fund which the elegant giant had set up for needy
kids. While a capacity crowd joined the organist's
rousing rendition of "He's a Jolly Good Fellow",
thieves were ransacking the Beliveau home across the
river in Longueuil.

March 31 and April 4—Canadiens drop two games to
Boston Bruins as the schedule ends, making obvious
what practically everybody suspected—Canadiens
would be no match for the swashbuckling Bruins in
the NHL playoff quarter-finals. After setting 34 different scoring records, Bruins were favoured to eliminate Canadiens in five games.

April 7—As expected, Bruins win the opener but
Canadiens go down in respectable fashion, 3–1. *The
Sporting News* carries a feature titled: "There's No
Way To Stop Bobby Orr."

April 8—The Bruins, leading 5–1 midway in the game,
run into a Canadien tornado of fire-wagon hockey
that nets six goals in a row and wins for them, 7–5.
Beliveau ignited the fuse with two goals, two assists.

April 10—The bookies begin to fret as Canadiens take
the series lead with a 3–1 win in Montreal. But betting
odds still favour Bruins—how could such power be
throttled? No way.

April 11-13—Bruins score emphatic back-to-back wins,
5–2, and 7–3, as their vaunted power—four 100-

point men, ten 20-plus goal scorers—pours it on. The bookies make them 4½-to-1 favorites.

April 15—Oops! Who exactly has the powerhouse? Canadiens send the Forum fans into the stratosphere with an 8–3 win and the series goes the limit . . . with the seventh and final fray on Boston ice.

April 18—Bruins take an early lead but the incredible Canadiens roar back with four goals to eliminate Bruins, 4–2. Bruins showered 48 shots on Ken Dryden, but even at that it was a fairly restful night— he had faced 56 in the fifth game. Boston had one comfort; they had witnessed what was rated the greatest upset in NHL history.

April 20—Canadiens open the semi-final series against Minnesota North Stars to win 7–2, without over exertion. It looks like a short series.

April 22—North Stars suddenly shine, win 6–3, and John Ferguson throws a tantrum, banging stick on boards and leaving the bench before the game has ended. Some writers recall that while Canadiens ended third in the East Division they would have ended fourth if both divisions had been united. Despite what they did to Bruins, they just weren't that good.

April 24—Controversy rages around Coach MacNeil, who ignores it as Canadiens win, 6–3.

April 25—What goes on here? North Stars win, 5–2.

April 27-29—With the series tied, Canadiens turn it on to win, 6–1, then end it in a 3–2 squeaker. Now for the Chicago Black Hawks.

May 4—The Stanley Cup finals open in Chicago with a thriller, as Jim Pappin's goal in the second overtime period sinks Les Habs.

May 6—Black Hawks do it again, 5–3, to take a commanding lead in the series shifting to Forum ice.

May 9-11—Again it proves the Year of the Underdog as Canadiens come back to even the series on Forum ice with 4–2 and 5–2 wins. The press boys have a lot of fun with rookie Rejean Houle (165 pounds), nicknamed the "Peanut", who had been assigned to shadow Bobby Hull. For example: "Peanut Drives Hull Nuts."

May 13—Back to Chicago where Hawks blank the Canadiens, 2-0, but a post-game eruption leaves the game secondary. Henri Richard blasts Coach Mac-Neil as "the worst coach I have ever played for in my career . . . an incompetent coach." Montreal Gazette's Ted Blackman added that the rebellion was widespread, that Pollock was left with the choice of trading a dozen players or of replacing the coach.

May 16—MacNeil keeps his cool despite a death threat that brought a 24-hour police guard extending even to the bench at game time. Richard says ruefully: "I should have kept my mouth shut." MacNeil says: "Let's play hockey." Canadiens, in keeping with their reputation for revelling in any kind of pressure, come from behind twice to beat Chicago, 4–3. The winner was a thriller with Frank Mahovlich setting up kid brother Pete; the two brothers hugged one another furiously for a full minute.

May 18—Again a series' seventh-game limit. Although Canadiens are on foreign ice the bookies place them 9-5 favourites. Hawks go ahead 2–0 and appear to have thrown up an impregnable defence, until halfway through the game Jacques Lemaire slaps a floater 80 feet; somehow Chicago goalie Tony Esposito misjudges the puck, flops to his knees as it goes in over his shoulder. Henri Richard's two goals win the game to give Dick (*New York News*) Young a heading for his column: "Henri Richard Wins Stanley Cup for the Worst Coach He Ever Played For." A medical bulletin added a remarkable item; Canadien defenceman Jacques Laperriere had played through most of the Chicago series with a broken arm!

May 19—Several thousand fans whoop it up at Montreal International Airport as the world champion Canadiens' "champagne flight" lands from Chicago about three a.m. They keep right on whooping; when the Victory Parade forms at noon in midsummer sun and heat, there are an estimated 500,000 lining the route through the major shopping district and down to the City Hall where Mayor Drapeau champagnes them some more. President David Molson's all-out Victory Dinner at the Queen Elizabeth Hotel gets underway just 21 hours after the underdog Canadiens had skated out onto the ice at Chicago Stadium. Winning the Stanley Cup doesn't lose its wingding celebration stimulus—for fans or players—even when it happens a record sixteenth time.

General Manager Sam Pollock missed the noon motor cavalcade but had one of his own. A deep-down, sweat-provoking horror of flying machines had him making two round trips to Minnesota and three to Chicago by auto. He got to the party just as the Molson family receiving line was dissolving. Minutes later I saw David Molson and Pollock in a head-to-head huddle at a lonely table in the far corner, talking intensely—not at all in the jubilant way of celebration.

Were they already discussing a potential trade? I don't doubt it. The restlessness of the Canadien front office has been a grossly underestimated factor in the team's unmatched history of success, and the 1971 triumph was an outstanding although not too apparent example.

Before each playoffs, the teams who make it have to file an eligibility list—usually naming up to 33 players whom they own and wish to be available for playing if needed. They don't all get into action; many practice but are in civvies at the games. For instance, Canadiens' No. 3 goalie, Phil Myre, never was in uniform during the 20 playoff games. But the 1971 eligibility list was significant: of the 31 players listed, an even dozen were not on the eligibility list of only two years before, 1969, when Canadiens won their previous Stanley Cup.

Typical, too, was the decision to use a raw, 21-year-old rookie, Rejean Houle from Rouyn, Quebec, developed by the Junior Canadiens, to smother the mighty Bobby Hull. Nobody can completely hold Hull from the scoring sheets, but he was contained enough by the bruised 165-pounder to give Canadiens a slight edge. The edge might not have existed if, for example, Canadiens had been forced to use Yvan Cournoyer primarily on anti-Hull duty. Cournoyer, fast approaching superstardom, emerged from the playoffs as a 10-goal scorer while assisting on 12 others.

Personally I am inclined to believe that the key deal transforming Canadiens from another potentially also-ran role in 1970-71 was the trade that got them the Big M, Frank Mahovlich. And, of course, the astounding decision to send rookie Ken Dryden into the nets for the entire 20-game playoff grind proved the icing on the cake. While Dryden was the shoo-in choice for the Smythe best-in-playoffs Trophy, the Big M set an NHL playoff record with 14 goals, and his 27 points tied the playoff record set the year before by Boston's Phil Esposito.

When Frank Mahovlich donned a Canadien sweater in mid-January of 1971, it was almost instantly apparent that a transformation had taken place. *The Hockey Pictorial's* Gil Smith headlined a lead feature:

"Has The 'Big M' Found Happiness At Last?"

It was a strange question, indeed, to ask about a player who has scored more than 400 goals and assisted on more than 400 others. But it was quite true that from the day in 1957 that he was lifted by Toronto Maple Leafs from junior stardom with Toronto St. Mike's, he had been an unhappy fella most of the way—moody, overcritical of himself, sensitive to fan displeasure to the point of nervous breakdown. Traded to Detroit and now to Montreal. But somehow a curtain lifted. He told me:

"The Canadiens are altogether different from any team I have ever known. There is a great sense of pride that one feels even in practices—somehow I'm back to the hockey feel I haven't felt since I was a junior. Being with the kid brother (Pete Mahovlich) is good but wheeling in with the likes of Jean Beliveau—my God he's good!—and the hellbent Yvan Cournoyer is excitement, real hockey excitement. My wife has always liked Montreal and I guess that has helped, too. . . ."

The night of February 11 at the Forum was one of the all-time most thrilling even for the Forum—the night that Belliveau scored three goals to hit the towering 500th-goal stratum. And the fans, most hockey-wise of any city in the world, were quick to give the Big M credit for playing his heart out to help. It was he who broke out of the Canadiens' end to lead a three-on-two attack over the Minnesota blue line that ended in Goal No. 500 for Jean. While Goal No. 499 went into the record book as "unassisted", it was Frank Mahovlich who played the key role by forcing Ted Harris (the ex-Canadien traded to Minnesota) to lose the puck in the Minnesota zone, then blocking off Harris to let Beliveau sweep in alone and score.

It was difficult to tell which of the two—Belliveau or Frank Mahovlich—was the happier. But the fans were quick to recognize the warming spirit of team play, particularly when Beliveau surged over to hug his opponent of so many bitter Toronto and Detroit games.

Afterwards, in the jubilant Directors' Room at the Forum, I remarked to the now retired, former general manager of Canadiens, Frank Selke: "When I see the way Frank Mahovlich is playing now I have to think he must have been worth the $1,000,000 offered for him nine years ago (1962) by Jim Norris."

It was no publicity stunt, as so many cynics maintained. I was there, at the annual All-Star Dinner in

Toronto, when the late owner of Chicago Black Hawks made the offer. Admittedly, Norris was feeling no pain but he never failed to back up an offer or a bet with a cheque—and, in profound awe, I held that cheque in my hot hands for an unbelieving look. The Leaf's brass, staggered by the unheard-of offer, at first accepted, then refused, but not before some backstage pressure I hadn't known about until Selke told me in 1971.

The Leafs were worried about the effect of any possible "welshing" accusation and knew that, for some reason, Selke of Canadiens was the only man who could talk to Norris when he was in an aggressive mood. Selke related how he was asked to go up to Norris's suite in the Royal York Hotel and ask him to call everything off—like a nice guy, please.

Selke made a diplomatic approach: "You know, Jim, no hockey player is worth a million dollars."

"That fuddling hockey player is," roared Norris. "I'm telling you, Frank, with him and Bobby Hull I'll have a dynasty underway in Chicago. Between your Canadiens in Montreal and my Hawks in Chicago we'll ride the Leafs right out of the league. . . ."

Selke sighed in recollection: "It began to make good listening but I suddenly realized why I was there and that I had better adopt another approach."

After letting Norris walk around the suite for a few minutes and pour himself a simmering-down belt, tee-totaller Selke interrupted quietly, "Why not face it, Jim, a million dollars is an awful lot of money."

Norris took a long quaff. "Look, Frank, I got 250 million fuddling dollars. What in hell would be the difference if I have 249?"

I hope Selke didn't tell me the story in confidence; it's too good to keep from the he-man history of the National Hockey League—and it does place a memorable estimate on the true value of the Big M, the biggest enigma the league has ever known. When his trade to

Canadiens was announced I felt the tide had changed for the Canadiens and, on a broadcast shortly afterwards on Vancouver's CKNW, was prompted to say: "The acquisition of Frank Mahovlich has made Canadiens an underdog prospect to win the 1971 Stanley Cup—Bruins or no Bruins." Nothing that happened subsequently prompted me to change; in the playoffs he was runner-up to Ken Dryden for the Smythe Trophy, but who could fault the selectors on that choice?

Dryden had accepted the mantle of Canadien goal-keeping immortals—all the way down from Vezina through the eras of other Canadiens who won the trophy named after him—George Hainsworth, Bill Durnan, Jacques Plante, Charlie Hodge, Gump Worsley, Rogatien Vachon. In the 20 playoff games Dryden played in 40 days, he faced 711 shots (286 by Boston alone) and allowed only 63 goals under the most intense pressure imaginable.

At the Victory Dinner in Montreal I asked President Molson when he had first heard of Ken Dryden. He thought for a moment. "When Claude Ruel came back from watching him play college hockey in the United States—it was Ruel's scouting report that got us interested."

But what other NHL club about to face the seemingly unbeatable Boston Bruins and knowing only too well that in the playoffs a goaler means 50 per cent of your team, would go with a six-game rookie? And would stick with him after losing the opener while keeping a former Vezina veteran, Rogatien Vachon, on the bench?

Actually, the six-foot-four, 23-year-old Dryden doesn't look like a rugged athlete; he looks more like a bemused legal beagle, which he is, or almost is. The distracting playoffs and accompanying travel caused a delay in taking his final law exams at McGill University. Through most of the Boston series he toted along some tomes on Trusts but confessed it was difficult to concentrate.

McGill informed him he could take the exams in the Fall and Ken sighed with relief; now he'd be able to rest his optics (he wears horn-rimmed glasses off the ice, contact lenses on the ice) for those 100-m.p.h. slapshots.

There is even a growing suspicion that the completely unflappable puck-stopper simply cannot see the length of the ice. This was borne out by a story told me by Dick Irvin, son of the late coach and now a topflight sportscaster in Montreal. After the final game in Chicago, the press bus had left for the airport and Irvin aimed for the players' bus. He found himself walking beside Dryden and Rogatien Vachon.

"Just how did Henri (Richard) score the winning goal?" Dryden asked Vachon, "I just couldn't make out what happened at the far end."

He should have had a good view because his defence was well up over the Canadien blue line and he was at ice level but, anyway, there was Vachon excitedly relating the dramatic approach to and scoring of the goal that copped the Cup. Dryden kept walking along, slightly stooped like a professor ambling through his garden, muttering, "Incredible!" He repeated it five times.

All in all, Ken Dryden struck us of the communications media as an enthusiastic fan deeply delighted to be getting in to see all the NHL classics for nothing. "No, I had never seen either Bobby Orr or Bobby Hull in the flesh until they were shooting at me."

A native of Islington, Ontario, he had attracted Canadien's scouting interest (Ruel) while attending Cornell University on a hockey scholarship. He was All-America three times and compiled a 76-4-1 record while helping Cornell to three eastern college titles and taking them into the NCAA three times—winning the national crown once. From there he went to the Canadian national team and Sam Pollock persuaded him to play part-time for the Montreal Voyageurs (Canadiens' American League farm club) while attending McGill

University. When the Canadiens ran into hot-and-cold performances from Vachon and Myre, Pollock called Dryden up to the Canadiens shortly before the March 7 deadline and eased him into the major league by playing him on the road against expansion teams. Dryden played in six regular schedule games before the playoffs and Canadiens won them all.

The decision to play him in playoff pressure—particularly against the fearsome firepower of the Boston Bruins —was still a gambling and courageous one. But the reasoning was that it would take Bruins a while to figure out this huge, unfamiliar goaler with a spectacular catching hand—after all, even if it was against much inferior shooting, Dryden had compiled a phenomenal 1.60 goals-against average at Cornell while making 1,987 saves, which indicated reflexes extraordinary. Perhaps, figured the Canadien brass, by the time the Bruins get him figured we'll have an edge. . . . It worked, not just for a game or two but for twenty.

What started as a gamble—after all, the scheduled season showed Canadiens were only the fourth-best team in the NHL—produced an astonishing super-goaler who failed to wilt even under a single-game, 56-shot bombardment by the Bruins.

It did something else—it added to the Montreal mystique that seems to carry her Canadien teams over and above heights to which their combined skills at that time could not reach.

Not world wars, nor depressions, nor burned-out rinks, nor harsh tragedies nor riots have been able to alter the hellbent-for-goals course of hockey's Flying Frenchmen, nor diminsh the vigour of their fans' chant, "Les Canadiens sont la!"

Of course, the cosmopolitan nature of Montreal injects a freewheeling atmosphere into almost its every project. The Canadiens have struck me as perhaps the most cosmopolitan thing about cosmopolitan Montreal. In a city predominantly French-Canadian and Catholic, the ownership through fifty-four years—like the playing rosters—has shown constant variations from French and Catholic and English and Protestant, or English and Catholic. One of the team's most respected coaches, Cecil Hart, was a Jew whose father, Dr. David A. Hart, donated the most prized trophy of them all—the Hart Trophy for the most valuable player.

New teams have come and gone from the National Hockey League scene—the Montreal Wanderers, the Quebec Bulldogs, the Hamilton Tigers, the Ottawa Senators, the Pittsburgh Pirates, the New York Americans, the Philadelphia Quakers, the Montreal Maroons. Others changed identities—Toronto's Arenas became the St. Pats, then the Maple Leafs; Detroits Falcons became the Red Wings. But Montreal's Canadiens, unchanging in style or name, whirled their way through the fifty-four years without missing a game.

Within that lifetime the National Hockey League has grown from a low-crowd and comparatively leaky-roof operation to one which, in 1970-71, saw fourteen teams of cities ranging from Atlantic to Pacific play to an overall 88.73 per cent of capacity. The older East Division had an overall of 97.36 despite including the two newest expansion clubs, which proved the unequalled appeal of hockey in the realm of pro sport. Vancouver played to 98 per cent of capacity, Buffalo to 85.9.

In terms of people, the 14-city total in paid admissions hit an all-time record total of 8,000,200. To those must be added the steadily growing television audience; the cliff-hanger seventh and last game of the final series at Chicago was picked up by the the CBS network in the United States, so a conservative estimate would place the audience at twelve million.

Contributing to this evergreen surge of success have been many factors from the ivory towers of management —National Hockey League headquarters down through the various clubs' front offices—to the players' benches. But the greatest single contribution to the continuing appeal of sport's most successful operation has been the fire-wagon style of hockey which Canadiens play on the road as well as at home.

The hockey world saw it anew in the 1971 playoffs when an inferior Canadien team refused to die, kept clawing back from behind and overcoming deficits as insurmountable as four goals. Perhaps the most awed comment of all came from an unusual source—one of the Canadiens themselves. Frank Mahovlich had just finished a half-season as a Canadien; 13½ seasons before had been spent as an arch-opponent of Canadiens while wearing the colours of Toronto Maple Leafs and Detroit Red Wings.

"It's an amazing thing," said the Big M, "in all those years of fighting Canadiens I thought of them only as waves of attackers but they actually show more defensive hockey than one imagines—in a way, they're an optical illusion but they sure are the spirit of hockey at its most exciting best."

Postscript to 1970-71

There were two particularly intriguing postscripts to the 1970-71 season, one from a column by Sports Editor Joe Falls of the *Detroit Free Press* and the other from a talk—or lecture?—delivered by goalie Ken Dryden in Chicago.

Falls, who must be regarded as a neutral observer, did a column titled: "Stanley Cup Finals A Flaming Spectacle."

He wrote that "long after the final score of the Stanley Cup final is forgotten and even after they sit in pubs and argue whether little Henri scored the winner on a forehand or backhand," his memories will remain of "the most exciting sports event I've covered in years . . . for this is some kind of hockey team, my friend, not the best of all time and perhaps not even the best of the season, but none, in all the history of this sport, displayed as much poise under pressure as did these Canadiens . . . watching Ken Dryden in awe, wondering how anyone just 23 years old could step in and play with Canadiens as if he had been with the team for years . . . not with Penguins, or North Stars, or even the Black Hawks . . . these were the Canadiens, the most fabled hockey team in the lore and legend of this sport . . . I felt just being there, how damned fortunate I felt to have the job I have. . . ."

Dryden, in Chicago to accept an automobile as side-gift to the Most Valuable Playoff Player award (Smythe Trophy), spoke of pressure:

"There was pressure in the first little league game I played as a six-year-old. There was pressure in the first college game and the first college playoffs, the first pro game and the Stanley Cup playoffs. I find pressure is a difficult, exciting, unusual situation."

The difference between tending goal for Cornell and Canadiens?

"In college hockey you have to concentrate for maybe only 10 minutes and the rest of the time you can let your mind wander. Up here (in the NHL) you have to concentrate a full 60 minutes, or you're beat. It's a faster game, faster shooting and a lot more difficult for a goalie."

Epilogue

Back in 1959, photographer (now photo editor) Louis Jaques of *Weekend Magazine* left me in London to do a colour feature on the Royal Family at Windsor Castle. He returned puzzled over a conversation with Queen Elizabeth about Montreal's Canadiens.

Eight years previously the then Princess Elizabeth, touring Canada with Prince Philip, had expressed a desire to see the Canadiens in action. Entirely in keeping with the team's French tradition, *Le Club de Hockey Canadien* and its fans promptly reacted with a dashing tribute to England's fair lady by shifting a scheduled Forum date with New York's Rangers to fit in with the date of the Princess's presence in Montreal on October 29, 1951. Recalling that night with photographer Jaques, the Queen spoke of "a wonderful Canadien player" whose name she couldn't remember. Jaques politely suggested that Her Majesty must be thinking of Maurice Richard?

"No," she said thoughtfully, "it was an interestingly different name—could it have been Busher?"

Jaques took a deep breath. "Could Your Majesty be thinking of Floyd (Busher) Curry?"

Delightedly, the Queen said that was the name and how was he doing? Barely managing to conceal his surprise, Jaques told her the Busher had just retired from professional hockey for a business career but later, in my London hotel room, Jaques exclaimed:

"Tell me, Andy, how in the world could anybody remember Busher and not remember Rocket Richard?"

For the answer to that one, research has to go backstage into the Canadiens' dressing-room on that Forum night.

The huge arena had been scrubbed and touched up with gay paints. A lush red carpet had been installed between the Royal Box and a special platform devised for her Royal Highness to walk out above the ice and shake hands with the opposing captains. The fifteen thousand rabid Montreal fans had been discreetly coached on behaviour for that one night and were models of graciousness. But down in the Canadiens' room, Coach Dick Irvin was frankly worried.

From long experience he had learned to sense the volcanic build-up caused by a period of frustration imposed by severe checking and close refereeing on his superstar. He felt the sullen Rocket was due to blast off and, shuddering at the thought that tonight could be the night, took a few of Richard's stalwart mates aside. Irvin ordered them to thwart any potential explosion in the bud.

Sure enough, within the opening five minutes of play, dignity went by the boards—in fact, the Rocket draped Ranger badman Lou Fontinato right over the boards and was shaking his gloves loose when three mates forcibly removed him beyond fistic reach of target. The Rocket's stunned surprise was obviously shared by the Rangers; amidst the distracting atmosphere Busher Curry romped to a hat-trick performance of three goals (and apparent immortality at Windsor Castle) as Canadiens won, 6-1.

Years later I told Busher (now Supervisor of Administration and Public Relations for the Canadiens as well

as Vice-President of International Fuel Inc. in Montreal)
about the conversation at the Castle.

He laughed: "To tell you the truth, I wasn't trying to
impress royalty that night as much as the coach. Irvin
had threatened to ship me down to Buffalo in the
minors."

The Busher, beyond flashing moments, was no star but
he was far better than an honest journeyman player. His
one hundred and five goals in six hundred and one
regular NHL games don't tell as much about him as his
twenty-three goals in ninety-one playoff-pressured games
while helping Canadiens win three Stanley Cups.

On reading the proofs, I find my book hasn't done
players of the Curry calibre justice.

By way of apology for brushing by so many gallant
guys to concentrate on the superstars I can only point out
that this was not meant to be an exhaustive history of the
Canadiens. It was intended purely as the story of
hockey's fabulous Flying Frenchmen and, just as winning
armies are identified solely by the names of their field
generals, I feel the unnamed warriors of all the great
Canadiens' teams right back to 1910 are proudly content
just to know they were there—in the era of the particular
superstar they helped boost into orbit.

We, high up in the Press Boxes, are inclined to get
dazzled by the stars. We may forget to mention you,
Busher baby, but you have been given something that
no typewriter has given us—the right to throw back your
shoulders and let the look of eagles gleam again in your
eyes as you tell your grandchildren:

"I was a Canadien!"

Andy O'Brien

Records

Canadiens' Roll of Honour

Following is a complete list of the personnel of Canadiens' teams through the history of the National Hockey League who have won the world's championships, special awards or election to the Hockey Hall of Fame.

Canadiens' Stanley Cup Teams

The Stanley Cup, symbolic of the world's hockey championship, has been won a record sixteen times by the Montreal Canadiens during the National Hockey League's first fifty-four years (and once before the NHL).

It is the oldest trophy competed for by professional athletes in North America, donated for presentation to the amateur hockey champions of Canada in 1893 by Lord Stanley of Preston and son of the Earl of Derby. Since 1910 when the National Hockey Association, predecessor of the NHL, took possession of the cup, it has been the symbol of professional hockey supremacy. What began with an investment of ten pounds ($48.67 at the time) by Lord Stanley now represents $157,500 for dividing among the personnel of the team that wins it each spring. Alterations on the cup's rising structure have cost $6,000 and engraving the winner's names through the decades has amounted to $8,250 more.

Here are the rosters of the 17 Canadiens' teams etched on the Stanley Cup:

1923/24 *Montreal Canadiens*—Georges Vezina, Sprague Cleghorn, Billy Coutu, Howie Morenz, Aurel Joliat, Billy Boucher, Jean Matz, Odie Cleghorn, Sylvio Mantha, J. (Curley) Hedley, Leo Dandurand (manager-coach).

1929/30 *Montreal Canadiens*—George Hainsworth, Marty Burke, Sylvio Mantha, Howie Morenz, Bert McCaffrey, Aurel Joliat, Albert Leduc, Pit Lepine, Wildor Larochelle, Nick Wasnie, Gerald Carson, Armand Mondou, Georges Mantha, Gus Rivers, Leo Dandurand (manager), Cecil Hart (coach), Ed Dufor (trainer).

1930/31 *Montreal Canadiens*—George Hainsworth, W. Larochelle, Marty Burke, Sylvio Mantha, Howie Morenz, Johnny Gagnon, Aurel Joliat, Albert Leduc, Pit Lepine, Nick Wasnie, Bert McCaffrey, Armand Mondou, Georges Mantha, Art Lesieur, Gus Rivers, Leo Dandurand (manager), Cecil Hart (coach), Ed Dufor (trainer).

1943/44 *Montreal Canadiens*—Toe Blake, Maurice Richard, Elmer Lach, Ray Getliffe, Murph Chamberlain, Phil Watson, Emile Bouchard, Glen Harmon, Buddy O'Connor, Jerry Heffernan, Mike McMahon, Leo Lamoureux, Fernand Majeau, Bob Fillion, Bill Durnan, Tommy Gorman (manager), Dick Irvin (coach), Ernie Cook (trainer).

1945/46 *Montreal Canadiens*—Elmer Lach, Toe Blake, Maurice Richard, Bob Fillion, Dutch Hiller, Murph Chamberlain, Ken Mosdell, Buddy O'Connor, Glen Harmon, Jim Peters, Emile Bouchard, Billy Reay, Ken Reardon, Leo Lamoureux, Frank Eddolls, Gerry Plamondon, Bill Durnan, Tommy Gorman (manager) Dick Irvin (coach), Ernie Cook (trainer).

1952/53 *Montreal Canadiens*—Gerry McNeil, Jacques Plante, Doug Harvey, Butch Bouchard, Tom Johnson, Dollard St. Laurent, Bud MacPherson, Maurice Richard, Elmer Lach, Bert Olmstead, Bernie Geoffrion, Floyd Curry, Paul Masnick, Billy Reay, Dickie Moore, Ken Mosdell, Dick Gamble, Johnny McCormack, Lorne Davis, Calum MacKay, Eddie Mazur, Frank Selke (manager), Dick Irvin (coach), Hector Dubois (trainer).

1955/56 *Montreal Canadiens*—Jacques Plante, Doug Harvey, Butch Bouchard, Bob Turner, Tom Johnson, Jean-Guy Talbot, Dollard St. Laurent, Jean Beliveau, Bernie Geoffrion, Bert Olmstead, Floyd Curry, Jackie Leclair, Maurice Richard, Dickie Moore, Henri Richard, Ken Mosdell, Don Marshall, Claude Provost, Frank Selke (manager), Toe Blake (coach), Hector Dubois (trainer).

1956/57 *Montreal Canadiens*—Jacques Plante, Gerry McNeil, Doug Harvey, Tom Johnson, Bob Turner, Dollard St. Laurent, Jean-Guy Talbot, Jean Beliveau, Bernie Geoffrion, Floyd Curry, Dickie Moore, Maurice Richard, Claude Provost, Bert Olmstead, Henri Richard, Phil Goyette, Don Marshall, André Pronovost, Connie Broden, Frank Selke (manager), Toe Blake (coach), Hector Dubois (trainer).

1957/58 *Montreal Canadiens*—Jacques Plante, Gerry McNeil, Doug Harvey, Tom Johnson, Bob Turner, Dollard St. Laurent, Jean-Guy Tabot, Albert Langlois, Jean Beliveau, Bernie Geoffrion, Maurice Richard, Dickie Moore, Claude Provost, Bert Olmstead, Henri Richard, Marcel Bonin, Phil Goyette, Don Marshall, André Pronovost, Connie Broden, Frank Selke (manager), Toe Blake (coach), Hector Dubois (trainer).

1958/59 *Montreal Canadiens*—Jacques Plante, Charlie Hodge, Doug Harvey, Tom Johnson, Bob Turner, Jean-Guy Talbot, Albert Langlois, Bernie Geoffrion, Ralph Backstrom, Bill Hicke, Maurice Richard, Dickie Moore, Claude Provost, Ab McDonald, Henri Richard, Marcel Bonin, Phil Goyette, Don

Marshall, André Pronovost, Jean Beliveau, Frank Selke (manager), Toe Blake (coach), Hector Dubois (trainer).

1959/60 *Montreal Canadiens*—Jacques Plante, Charlie Hodge, Doug Harvey, Tom Johnson, Bob Turner, Jean-Guy Talbot, Albert Langlois, Ralph Backstrom, Jean Beliveau, Marcel Bonin, Bernie Geoffrion, Phil Goyette, Bill Hicke, Don Marshall, Ab McDonald, Dickie Moore, André Pronovost, Claude Provost, Henri Richard, Maurice Richard, Frank Selke (manager), Toe Blake (coach), Hector Dubois, Larry Aubut (trainers).

1964/65 *Montreal Canadiens*—Lorne Worsley, Charlie Hodge, Jean-Claude Tremblay, Ted Harris, Jean-Guy Talbot, Terry Harper, Jacques Laperrière, Jean Gauthier, Noel Picard, Jean Beliveau, Ralph Backstrom, Dick Duff, Claude Larose, Yvan Cournoyer, Claude Provost, Bobby Rousseau, Henri Richard, Dave Balon, John Ferguson, Gord Berenson, Jim Roberts, Toe Blake (coach), Sam Pollock (general manager), Larry Aubut, Andy Galley (trainers).

1965/66 *Montreal Canadiens*—Lorne Worsley, Charlie Hodge, Jean-Claude Tremblay, Ted Harris, Jean-Guy Talbot, Terry Harper, Jacques Laperrière, Noel Price, Jean Beliveau, Ralph Backstrom, Dick Duff, Claude Larose, Yvan Cournoyer, Claude Provost, Bobby Rousseau, Henri Richard, Dave Balon, John Ferguson, Leon Rochefort, Jim Roberts, Toe Blake (coach), Sam Pollock (general manager), Larry Aubut, Andy Galley (trainers).

1967/68 *Montreal Canadiens*—Lorne Worsley, Rogatien Vachon, Jacques Laperriere, Jean-Claude Tremblay, Ted Harris, Serge Savard, Terry Harper, Carol Vadnais, Jean Beliveau, Gilles Tremblay, Ralph Backstrom, Dick Duff, Claude Larose, Yvan Cournoyer, Claude Provost, Bobby Rousseau, Henri Richard, John Ferguson, Danny Grant, Jacques Lemaire, Mickey Redmond, Toe Blake (coach), Sam Pollock (general manager), Larry Aubut, Ed Palchak (trainers).

1968-69 *Montreal Canadiens*—Lorne Worsley, Rogatien Vachon, Jacques Laperriere, Jean-Claude Tremblay, Ted Harris, Serge Savard, Terry Harper, Larry Hillman, Jean Beliveau, Ralph Backstrom, Dick Duff, Yvan Cournoyer, Claude Provost, Bobby Rousseau, Henri Richard, John Ferguson, Christian Bordeleau, Mickey Redmond, Jacques Lemaire, Lucien Gernier, Tony Esposito (spare goaltender), Claude Ruel (coach), Sam Pollock (general manager), Larry Aubut, Ed Palchak (trainers).

1970/71 *Montreal Canadiens*—Ken Dryden, Rogatien Vachon, Jacques Laperriere, Jean-Claude Tremblay, Serge Savard, Terry Harper, Jean Beliveau, Yvan Cournoyer, Henri Richard, John Ferguson, Jacques Lemaire, Claude Larose, Leon Rochefort, Guy Lapointe, Frank Mahovlich, Peter Mahovlich, Pierre Bouchard, Marc Tardiff, Rejean Houle, Phil Roberto, Larry Pleau, Bobby Sheehan, Charles Lefley, Bob Murdoch, Phil Myre (spare goaler), Al MacNeil (coach), Sam Pollock (general manager), Yvon Belanger and Ed Palchak (trainers).

and the pre-N.H.L. Stanley Cup team:

1915/16 *Montreal Canadiens*—Georges Vezina, Bert Corbeau, Jack Laviolette, Newsy Lalonde, Louis Berlinguette, Goldie Prodgers, Howard McNamara, Didier Pitre, Skene Ronan, Amos Arbour, Skinner Poulin, Jack Fournier, George Kennedy (manager).

Prince of Wales Trophy
This trophy, donated by His Royal Highness in 1924, is presented each year to the team finishing in first place in the East Division. With it goes $52,500 for division among team personnel.

Canadiens have won it a record 15 times. The years were: 1925, 1944, 1945, 1946, 1947, 1956, 1958, 1959, 1960, 1961, 1962, 1964, 1966, 1968 and 1969.

NHL Scoring Champions

The scoring champion is determined at the end of the regular schedule (playoff games don't count) by totalling goals and assists (one point each). If more than one player ends with the same total, the one with the most actual goals-scored wins the award. If still tied, it goes to the player with the fewer games played. If still tied, it goes to the player who scored first during the season.

Since 1947, the Art Ross Trophy (presented by Arthur Howie Ross, former manager-coach of the Boston Bruins) goes annually to the champ. Today finds cash added; $1,000 to the overall winner and overall runner-up gets $500. Also, the leader and runner-up at the end of each half of the season get $500 and $250 respectively.

The championship has been won thirteen times by Canadien players—a record of wins unmatched by any other club:

1917/18	Joe Malone	1947/48	Elmer Lach
1918/19	Newsy Lalonde	1954/55	Bernard Geoffrion
1920/21	Newsy Lalonde	1955/56	Jean Beliveau
1927/28	Howie Morenz	1957/58	Dickie Moore
1930/31	Howie Morenz	1958/59	Dickie Moore
1938/39	Toe Blake	1960/61	Bernard Geoffrion
1944/45	Elmer Lach		

Hart Memorial Trophy

The Hart Trophy goes "to the player adjudged to be most valuable to his team." Winner is selected by the Professional Hockey Writers' Association at the end of the regular season and gets $1,500. Runner-up receives $750.

The trophy is linked with Canadien history in that its original donor was Dr. David A. Hart, father of Cecil Hart, manager-coach of the Canadiens during eight seasons and part of a ninth in the period between 1925 and 1939.

It has been won a record 13 times by Canadien players:

1926/27	Herb Gardiner	1944/45	Elmer Lach
1927/28	Howie Morenz	1946/47	Maurice Richard
1930/31	Howie Morenz	1955/56	Jean Beliveau
1931/32	Howie Morenz	1960/61	Bernard Geoffrion
1933/34	Aurel Joliat	1961/62	Jacques Plante

1936/37 Babe Siebert   1963/64 Jean Beliveau
1938/39 Toe Blake

Vezina Trophy

Like the Hart Trophy, the Vezina Trophy is linked with Canadiens' history. This top goaling award was presented to the National Hockey League in 1926/27 by three former owners of the Canadiens (Leo Dandurand, Louis Letourneau and Joe Cattarinich) in memory of Georges Vezina, famed goalkeeper of Canadiens who collapsed during an NHL game on November 28, 1925, and died of tuberculosis a few months later.

Until recent seasons the award went simply to the goaler who has played the most games for the team with the least goals scored against it. Basically, the condition is unchanged but the new definition recognizes the two-goaler era, since all teams must dress two goalers it is now stipulated that the award goes to the goaler or goalers having played a minimum twenty-five games for the team with the fewest goals against it. (Typical example was the joint award in 1965/66 to Lorne Worsley and Charlie Hodge who appeared in fifty-one and twenty-six games respectively during the seventy-game schedule—relieving one another during the course of seven games.)

To the overall winner goes $1,500, runner-up $750. Also to the leader at the end of the first half goes $250 and the same to the second-half leader.

In fitting tribute to their own Hall-of-Famer, goaler Vezina, Canadien puck-stoppers have dominated with 18 wins.

1926/27 George Hainsworth	1956/57 Jacques Plante
1927/28 George Hainsworth	1957/58 Jacques Plante
1928/29 George Hainsworth	1958/59 Jacques Plante
1943/44 Bill Durnan	1959/60 Jacques Plante
1944/45 Bill Durnan	1961/62 Jacques Plante
1945/46 Bill Durnan	1963/64 Charlie Hodge
1946/47 Bill Durnan	1965/66 Lorne Worsley,
1948/49 Bill Durnan	Charlie Hodge
1949/50 Bill Durnan	1967/68 Lorne Worsley
1955/56 Jacques Plante	Rogatien Vachon

Calder Memorial Trophy

The Calder Trophy is awarded annually "to the player selected as the most proficient in his first year of competition in the National Hockey League" by a poll of the Professional Hockey Writers' Association. A winner cannot have played more than 25 games in any single preceding season nor in six or more games in each of any two preceding seasons. With the award goes $1,500 to the winner and $750 to the runner-up.

The trophy is called after the late Frank Calder, first president of the NHL and holder of that office until his death in 1943. He originated the trophy in 1936/37, the NHL continued it after he died.

The trophy has been won five times by Canadien players.

1940/41	John Quilty	1961/62	Bobby Rousseau
1951/52	Bernard Geoffrion	1963/64	Jacques Laperrière
1958/59	Ralph Backstrom		

James Norris Memorial Trophy

The Norris Trophy goes annually "to the defence player who demonstrates throughout the season the greatest all-round ability in that position". Selection is made by a poll of the Professional Hockey Writers' Association. The winner gets $1,500 and the runner-up $750.

The trophy was presented in 1953 by the four children of the late James Norris, former owner-president of the Detroit Red Wings.

The brief history of the award has been dominated by Canadien players, who have won it eight times:

1954/55	Doug Harvey	1958/59	Tom Johnson
1955/56	Doug Harvey	1959/60	Doug Harvey
1956/57	Doug Harvey	1960/61	Doug Harvey
1957/58	Doug Harvey	1965/66	Jacques Laperrière

Lady Byng Memorial Trophy

This award goes annually "to the player adjudged to have exhibited the best type of sportsmanship and gentlemanly conduct combined with a high standard of playing ability" from a poll by the Professional Hockey Writers' Association. With it goes $1,500 to the winner and $750 to the runner-up.

The trophy was originated in 1925 by Lady Byng, wife of Canada's Governor-General at the time. It has been won once by a Canadien:

1945/46   Toe Blake

Conn Smythe Trophy

This is an annual award "to the most valuable player for his team in the entire playoffs" as selected by the League Governors (or representatives) at the conclusion of the final playoff game. Winner also gets $1,500.

The trophy was presented by Maple Leaf Gardens in 1964 to honour Conn Smythe, former coach, manager, president and owner-governor of Toronto Maple Leafs and now honorary life governor.

It has been won three times by Canadien players:

1964/65 Jean Beliveau   1968/69 Serge Savard
1970/71 Ken Dryden

Canadiens Who Made the All-Stars

Voting for the N.H.L. All-Star Team is conducted among members of the Professional Hockey Writers' Association in the 14 cities at the end of the regular schedule. Each man on the First Team gets $2,000, on the Second Team $1,000.

Following is a list of the First and Second teams since their inception in 1930-31.

1930/31	1st Team	Howie Morenz, Aurel Joliat
	2nd Team	Sylvio Mantha
1931/32	1st Team	Howie Morenz
	2nd Team	Sylvio Mantha, Aurel Joliat
1932/33	2nd Team	Howie Morenz
1933/34	2nd Team	Aurel Joliat
1934/35	2nd Team	Aurel Joliat
1935/36	2nd Team	Wilf Cude
1936/37	1st Team	Babe Siebert
	2nd Team	Wilf Cude
1937/38	1st Team	Babe Siebert
	2nd Team	Toe Blake

1938/39	1st Team	Toe Blake
1939/40	1st Team	Toe Blake
1943/44	1st Team	Bill Durnan
	2nd Team	Emile Bouchard, Elmer Lach, Maurice Richard
1944/45	1st Team	Bill Durnan, Elmer Lach, Maurice Richard, Toe Blake, Emile Bouchard
	2nd Team	Glen Harmon
1945/46	1st Team	Bill Durnan, Emile Bouchard, Maurice Richard
	2nd Team	Kenny Reardon, Elmer Lach, Toe Blake.
1946/47	1st Team	Bill Durnan, Kenny Reardon, Emile Bouchard, Maurice Richard
1947/48	1st Team	Elmer Lach, Maurice Richard
	2nd Team	Kenny Reardon
1948/49	1st Team	Bill Durnan, Maurice Richard
	2nd Team	Glen Harmon, Kenny Reardon
1949/50	1st Team	Bill Durnan, Kenny Reardon, Maurice Richard
1950/51	2nd Team	Maurice Richard
1951/52	1st Team	Doug Harvey, Elmer Lach
	2nd Team	Maurice Richard
1952/53	1st Team	Doug Harvey
	2nd Team	Gerry McNeil, Bert Olmstead, Maurice Richard
1953/54	1st Team	Doug Harvey, Ken Mosdell
	2nd Team	Maurice Richard
1954/55	1st Team	Doug Harvey, Jean Beliveau, Maurice Richard
	2nd Team	Ken Mosdell, Bernard Geoffrion
1955/56	1st Team	Jacques Plante, Doug Harvey, Maurice Richard, Jean Beliveau
	2nd Team	Tom Johnson, Bert Olmstead
1956/57	1st Team	Doug Harvey, Jean Beliveau
	2nd Team	Jacques Plante, Maurice Richard
1957/58	1st Team	Doug Harvey, Henri Richard, Dickie Moore
	2nd Team	Jacques Plante, Jean Beliveau

1958/59	1st Team	Jacques Plante, Tom Johnson, Dickie Moore, Jean Beliveau
	2nd Team	Doug Harvey, Henri Richard
1959/60	1st Team	Doug Harvey, Jean Beliveau
	2nd Team	Jacques Plante, Bernard Geoffrion
1960/61	1st Team	Doug Harvey, Jean Beliveau, Bernard Geoffrion
	2nd Team	Henri Richard, Dickie Moore
1961/62	1st Team	Jacques Plante, Jean-Guy Talbot
1962/63	2nd Team	Henri Richard
1963/64	2nd Team	Charlie Hodge, Jean Beliveau, Jacques Laperriere
1964/65	1st Team	Claude Provost, Jacques Laperrière
	2nd Team	Charlie Hodge
1965/66	1st Team	Jacques Laperrière
	2nd Team	Lorne Worsley, Jean Beliveau, Bobby Rousseau
1967/68	1st Team	Lorne Worsley
	2nd Team	J. C. Tremblay
1968/69	2nd Team	Jean Beliveau, Ted Harris, Yvan Cournoyer
1969/70	2nd Team	J. Laperriere
1970/71	1st Team	J. C. Tremblay
	2nd Team	Yvan Cournoyer

Canadiens in the Hockey Hall of Fame

Located at the Canadian National Exhibition Park on the shore of Lake Ontario in Toronto, the Hockey Hall of Fame Building was formally opened on August 26, 1961, by the Prime Minister of Canada, John F. Diefenbaker.

Election as player, executive or as referee comes for distinguished service to hockey and stresses integrity, character and contribution to team as well as—in the case of former players—playing ability.

The conclusion of the National Hockey League's fifty-fourth season found 175 named to the Hall of Fame; twenty-nine of them have served the Montreal Canadiens as exec-

utives or players or both. Alphabetically listed, with asterisk
marking the deceased, are:

   Blake, Hector (Toe)
   Bouchard, Emile Joseph (Butch)
   *Cleghorn, Sprague
   *Dandurand, Joseph Viateur (Leo)
   Durnan, William Ronald (Bill)
   Gardiner, Herbert Martin (Herb)
   *Gorman, Thomas Patrick (Tommy)
   *Hainsworth, George
   *Hall, Joseph Henry
   *Irvin, James Dickenson (Dick)
   Johnson, Tom
   Joliat, Aurel
   Lach, Elmer James
   *Lalonde, Edouard Charles (Newsy)
   *Laviolette, Jean Baptiste (Jack)
   *Malone, Joseph (Joe)
   Mantha, Sylvio
   *McNamara, George
   *Morenz, Howie
   *Northey, William M.
   *O'Brien, John Ambrose
   *Patrick, Frank
   *Pitre, Didier (Pit)
   *Raymond, Senator Donat
   Reardon, Kenneth Joseph
   Richard, Joseph Henri Maurice (Rocket)
   Selke, Frank J.
   *Siebert, Albert C. (Babe)
   *Vezina, Georges